By

FLOYD
SHUSTER
MAINE

LONE EAGLE

...The White Sioux

Floyd S. Maine

THE UNIVERSITY OF NEW MEXICO PRESS

Albuquerque - 1956

128488

DEDICATED
to the MEMORY OF MY PARENTS

Rev. George W. Maine and Emma (Shuster) Maine,
Pioneer missionaries in the West

AND TO MY SON AND DAUGHTER

Merle Eagle and Shirley Juanita,
who were born too late to know the West
as it was

Publisher's Foreword

LONE EAGLE, THE WHITE SIOUX, WAS NEITHER THE FIRST NOR the only white child to be adopted into an Indian tribe. However, the true story of this child of missionary parents who lost their lives ministering to the needs of the Oglala Sioux of Dakota during a smallpox epidemic, rivals the most imaginative novel.

The tiny baby, adopted by Chief Big Elk and his wife, "Ma-pi Winna" (Cloud Woman), was given the name "Wamble Ish-na-la" (Lone Eagle), and thus lost all identification with his white ancestry. Until twelve years of age he believed himself to be an Oglala Sioux Indian.

Meeting of the brothers, Floyd Shuster Maine (author of this book), and Lone Eagle, neither of whom knew of the other's existence, is a narrative worth reading. But the real value of this biography is the insight into the Indian life it reveals. Only a child so reared could give so accurately the Indian's viewpoints, customs, and history.

Here may be found the Indians' own version of Custer's last fight, as related to Lone Eagle by the chiefs and warriors involved.

Several chapters, written by Lone Eagle himself, draw vivid pictures of the life and training of an Indian boy. He retells stories and legends of the Oglalas—of the buffalo hunts, the effect of the coming of the white men on Indian life—as told him by Chief Big Elk, his father; and others who thus passed on the history and legends of their proud heritage.

We recommend this book to all desiring a clearer understanding of the Indians and their relations with the white people.

Foreword

I HAVE WAITED LONG FOR THIS STORY TO BE WRITTEN. THE co-author of this book is one of the very few persons living today whose own personal experience, gained from long years of actual living in the tepees of the Sioux — as one of them — has given him a true knowledge of the real Indian. I know of no other person who can write with more knowledge and understanding of my people.

It is a great honor to write a word of introduction for this book, a privilege I appreciate very deeply, for I have had experiences in life somewhat similar to that of Lone Eagle.

The unusual life of Lone Eagle, a white man, as authentically related in the following pages, presents an important fundamental aspect of the differences between the two races — the white and the red.

Lone Eagle, in later years, received training and education among his own people; nevertheless, his knowledge of the psychology of the tribe, which molded his early life, makes him still remain a proud member.

This strange and unusual experience of a lone white child, who grew up among the Sioux Indians, as related in this book, serves to promote better understanding between the two races.

HENRY STANDING BEAR
Chief of Sioux Tribes

April 30, 1950

[Chief Henry Standing Bear, "Mato Najin," was a member of one of the first groups of Indian boys ever to be sent to the Carlisle Indian School — 1880 — from the Sioux reservations of the West. He died October 17, 1953.]

Contents

Chapter I

The Old Homestead

THE PIONEER IS A MAN OF ADVENTURE, WITHOUT WHOM NO NEW country would ever have been explored or made possible for settlement and permanent habitation. It was the spirit of adventure and a love of freedom that brought our forefathers to the eastern shores of America. This same inherited spirit urged their sons and daughters to seek new and less populated areas, in order to establish homes for their families. Their first settlements necessarily were close to the place of original landing and, as population increased and values advanced in the settled communities along the eastern coast, this same love of adventure brought caravans of pioneer settlers, pushing new frontiers ever toward the great West.

In one of these rock-strewn and picturesque valleys of northern New Jersey, in the county of Sussex, came a settlement of pious Dutch and German immigrants from the valley of the Rhine. They built a stone grist mill on the banks of Paulins Kill, and soon scattered homes were erected in the snug little valley around the mill, and the settlement was given the serene and peaceful name of Stillwater.

Among the first families to take up permanent residence along this picturesque little stream, was Johannes Henri Shuster and his wife, Marie, whose German-inscribed headstones may still be seen in the old stone-walled cemetery adjoining the village, although the moss-covered stones were placed there nearly two centuries ago.

In their wake came the proud and pious Jacob Maine, who settled on a plantation of some four hundred acres, where his nine stalwart sons and daughters grew up in their spacious twenty-room home of gray cut limestone. Old Jacob, the immigrant, was justly proud of his ancestry. His family had claimed title to a vast landed estate along the River Rhine since the sixteenth century and, if that was not enough to be proud of, he had documents to show that, in Normandy, his regal ancestors traced their lineage to Baron Geoffrey de Mayenne, who built the great stone Castle d'Mayenne along the River Mayenne in the beginning of the tenth century.

Jacob was a God-fearing man and most strict in his religious beliefs. His word was his bond and no man doubted his sincerity. It is no great wonder that, out of my grandfather's family of nine, my father should choose the ministry as his career.

He had recently been graduated from the state university, and had married the only daughter of the late Jacob Shuster. My mother was a graduate nurse and my father was rector of a small parish for a number of years following his marriage. On several occasions he had engaged as helper Rev. Chief Amos White Feather, an educated Sioux Indian. During their acquaintance my father became interested in White Feather and his glowing accounts of life among his tribesmen and, being fascinated with the idea of adventure in a new and little-known part of our country, he and my mother made serious plans to go west.

I was their only child and was then five years old. As my parents were desirous of giving me the best available education, it was decided that I should stay with my aunt and uncle in New Jersey and attend school, with the promise that my parents would return in three years. I did not realize then that I would never see them again. So, with much preparation and many tearful adieus, my parents departed for the West to become missionaries among the Sioux tribes of the Dakotas.

Chapter II

Coming of the Black Robes

SOME TWELVE WINTERS AFTER LONG HAIR GEN. GEORGE A. CUSTER
had fought his people on the Little Big Horn, in Montana,
Chief "Un-pan Tan-ka" (Big Elk) and his band were living
between the Missouri River and the Black Hills country in
South Dakota. The buffalo had been driven off the plains and
wantonly killed by the paleface hunters merely for their hides.

The Teton and Oglala Sioux then occupied most of the territory west of the Missouri River, in Dakota. Besides the few
provisions that were given them by the government from the
various agencies, they fished, trapped, and hunted for a living,
moving from place to place along streams and in the hills in
quest of fish and game.

While Chief Big Elk's band was camped on the White
River, waiting for the warm spring to come, several of them
had gone to the agency with their winter's catch of hides.
Their trader, Antone Renville, a French and Sioux half-
blood, had gone with them and would return with many
freight wagons of store articles for the Indians.

One day in May (the Green Grass Moon) Antone and his
freight-wagon teams were seen coming over the hills from the
south, followed by several Indians on horseback and a new,
white-canvas-covered wagon. On the front seat were two
strangers, a tall white man of medium weight, wearing a long,

3

black coat and a black, broad-brimmed hat. Beside him was a woman somewhat shorter in height, and of slightly stouter build. She wore a long black dress and a bonnet of the same material. In the wagon were several trunks, well-roped cases, and leather handbags. When they reached the camp, the Indians were informed that the two strangers were missionaries from the land toward the rising sun.

At first they lived in the lodge of Antone, the trader, and his half-Indian wife, but later they were given a lodge of their own. When possible, the Black Robes, as the Indians called them, built and occupied small cabins of pine or cottonwood logs along the small streams where the Indian camps were set up. If no logs could be found for this purpose, the missionaries lived in a canvas tepee like the Indians.

For two summers and one winter the missionaries had lived among Big Elk's people. The winter had been long and cold, and wild game had been scarce. It was now the month of "Wi-wa-zu-pi" (October), the Falling-Leaf-Moon, and Big Elk decided to move the camp to the Black Hills, where game was reported plentiful and good grass and shelter for their ponies could be had. They soon reached their new campsite and the hunters were sent out immediately in search of wild game for their winter store.

It was not long after their arrival when a tiny white papoose had come to gladden the lodge of the palefaces. After several days, many came to see the new white baby and bring him presents in token of their friendship. The hunters began to return with many deer, elk, antelope, and fowl, which the Indian women dressed—the hides they tanned to be used for moccasins and clothing.

The gods had been good to their red children and had given them plenty of mountain berries, meat, and furs. "Ta-tan-ka Na-zene" (Standing Buffalo), the tribal medicine man, had made good medicine and was now making ready for a feast and dance to the gods of the chase.

However, the two missionaries were not a little concerned over a score or more of the band who had what they thought to be a light form of smallpox. More people came down with it, and soon many lodges contained men, women, and children victims of the disease. As soon as the missionaries found out that it really was smallpox, they took their infant son to the lodge of "Mah-pi Winna" (Cloud Woman), the chief's wife, who cared for him while the white woman and her husband cared for the sick. They worked for many days but the disease steadily spread.

Days and weeks went by, many more took sick and several died. The missionary and his wife doctored and worked all through each day taking but little rest during the night, but by the time spring had come again over one hundred had died.

The worst of the disease passed; fewer were now sick, and deaths were less frequent. Soon there were no new cases. Several more died, but most of the sick were recovering. One day when nearly the last sick person was able to be out, the camp crier went through the village telling his people that their beloved paleface friends had been stricken with the dreaded disease. Helping hands came from many lodges, but no one had worked with the sick as they had. Day and night, men and women cared for them, doing everything in their power for their comfort and recovery, but not many days passed until the news went from lodge to lodge that the white woman had died, and before another week had passed the grief-stricken camp had buried both of their ever true and faithful friends.

After the death of the two missionaries, the white boy was kept in the chief's lodge and adopted as their own son. He was named "Wam-ble Ish-na-la" (Lone Eagle), after a brother of Big Elk, who had been killed in an Indian battle on the Little Big Horn. Lone Eagle grew up in the chief's tepee with "Ta-cin-ca Ska" (White Fawn), their niece, never knowing that he was not an Indian. As he grew up, he was taught all the craft of the young Indian boy. Big Elk made him bow and arrows, with which he learned to shoot birds and rabbits. He was taught how to fish and hunt, the art of scouting, how to track down horses and wild animals, and to follow all kinds of Indian trails; if he should chance to find a discarded moccasin along the trail he could tell to what tribe the wearer belonged by its design and style.

Lone Eagle often spent long winter evenings in the lodge of Hollow Horn Bear, best sign talker of all the Oglalas. Here he learned the Indian sign language of the western plains tribes, the unique and universal language as used by all the plains Indians, of whom the Crows, Blackfeet, Cheyennes, and Sioux were the most efficient. This most graceful and silent gesture language of the hands and body was the only means of communication as they did not understand each other's spoken language. He thus became a recognized sign talker in his band, and often acted as interpreter when meeting other tribes on the plains. When important messages were sent between bands or groups of Indians at distances too great to use the sign language, the fire and smoke signals, produced by means of a small fire and blanket, were used. This method was used in the earlier days to call tribes together for important council meetings, or among the individual Indians on hunting trips and war expeditions. Strange as it may seem to the unlearned observer, this sign language of the Western plains was as detailed in its use by an efficient sign talker as the spoken language itself, and valuable information was often sent across great distances in a matter of minutes by the experienced Indian with his sagebrush fire and blanket.

When in camp, Lone Eagle often watched his Indian mother as she tanned deer skins for clothing, made beaded moccasins, working pretty designs in colored porcupine quills, or made new tepee covers from canvas bought at the agencies, when buffalo skins could no longer be had.

Often in the evening as they sat in their lodge watching the dying embers of the smouldering fire, Big Elk and his warrior friends would smoke and tell stories of the long ago, when Big Elk was a young warrior and the buffalo roamed the vast plains in great herds, before the paleface had ventured far into the Sioux country. They would sit in the honored place in the tepee opposite the lodge entrance and after carefully unwrapping his beautifully decorated red stone pipe from its beaded elkskin pouch, Big Elk would slowly fill it with kin-ni-kin-nik tobacco and, holding the lighted pipe by its long wooden stem, would take several puffs. Then, with great ceremony, he would present the stem end of the pipe to the four cardinal directions, and one to the mother earth and again to "Wa-kan Tan-ka," the great spirit, after which he would pass the still lighted pipe to the warrior at his right, and so on, until all his guests had repeated the same ceremony. Then, after a pause, Big Elk would tell of some experience of his boyhood days on the warpath or on the trail in quest of the buffalo and other wild game which roamed the prairie and timbered lands in great numbers many summers ago.

Each in turn would tell of great feats of daring, and of wars against their enemies. Often someone would tell of long winters and great blizzards when much cold and suffering would be experienced by entire bands and tribes. Many stories were humorous, and everyone would laugh and shout with pleasure and excitement, but again some narratives would be very sad and even the stoic old men would be seen to shed tears and cover their faces in their grief. Many were the evenings that Lone Eagle heard their stories and legends which have been handed down from early generations by the Dakota people; true tales of Indian tribal life, never to be forgotten.

It was not until Lone Eagle was twelve years old that he knew that he was not a Sioux Indian or that Un-pan Tan-ka and Mah-pi Winna were not his real father and mother. One day some soldiers and missionaries visited their camp and asked the parents to send their children to a school which was located near Pine Ridge. As they entered the camp, the children ran to the lodges and stood looking at the strangers through the tent openings and from behind the tepees. After many friendly gestures, some of the larger boys came out to them. They noticed one of the boys had a very fair complexion and, instead of black braids, his hair was a dark brown. They began talking to him, but he understood no English. Through their interpreter they asked him who his parents were. He told them he was the son of Big Elk and Cloud Woman.

They believed Lone Eagle to be a white boy and not the son of the chief, and questioned Big Elk as to this white boy and where they got him. Fearing the white people might take him away Big Elk and Cloud Woman still claimed he was their own son. Others of the tribe were questioned and eventually they learned that he was the child of the missionaries who were buried in the Black Hills.

Although Lone Eagle learned then that he was not the son of Big Elk and Cloud Woman, to him they were his parents, for he had never known any other. They finally consented to let him go to school, but insisted that he still be their son and return to them. So he and several other children were taken to the reservation school.

He did not like this new life; it was not the free life of the noisy Indian camp. So one night he and several other boys stole out of the sleeping room through an open window and started for their homes. They walked and ran until the sun crept up over the hills. As it grew light they became frightened, expecting all the time to see the white teachers follow them and take them back, so they hid in a thick clump of willows, but as no one was seen, they continued on their way. When, at last, the boys reached home Lone Eagle entered the chief's lodge and greeted his parents; he told them that he did not like the white man's house and that he had run away. His mother then told him that he must return and would soon learn to like the white teachers and their school and would learn to understand and speak the white man's language. So once more Lone Eagle was taken to the agency school. He was very homesick for awhile, but as days passed he became more accustomed to this new life and soon made many friends in his new home.

Lone Eagle was at this school six years, learning the English language and the white man's way of living. He always returned to his Indian parents when school closed for a few months each year, with many wonderful tales about the interesting things he had learned. The world now seemed larger than he had ever dreamed it to be. As he grew older he often thought of the seldom-told story of his white parents, who had died among the Indians when he was but a few months old and how he had been adopted as the son of Chief Big Elk and his wife. He recalled that the white people at the Indian school did not have Indian names. Did he once have another name the same as these white teachers? But his Indian parents did not know or remember his white name, if they had ever heard it. They knew his parents only as the Black Robe missionaries. As to where they came from, no one knew, except that it was from the country toward the rising sun, near where the great white father of the palefaces lived.

In the fall of 1908, Lone Eagle took a trip to the Black Hills to visit the place of his birth and the graves of his parents. As he journeyed toward the west he saw, dotted over the broad prairies, many new farm houses where but a few years before was a vast expanse of rolling prairie land with perchance a ranch house here and there along the rivers and creeks. He had remembered these landmarks and camping places and, as he drew near the place where many graves lay on a long, flat, sunny slope, he noticed, a little to the south of the larger group of grass-covered graves, two small mounds, one on each side of a tall pine tree encircled by a ring of large stones. Thus they had been described to him by Mah-pi Winna but a short time before. He now remembered having camped with the Indians at the spring, but not until now did he know that his own mother and father had been buried there.

The world had been vague and unexplained to him. From this sacred spot he resolved to go and see more of it. He visited small bands of "I-san-ya-ti" (Santee), Dwellers-at-Knife-Lake, who lived on the Missouri River near the Chalk Rock Wall. And he journeyed to the east as far as the place where, according to Sioux legend, there was fought a great battle between the Sioux and the Ojibways, many many winters ago, long before our great grandfathers' time. So many braves from both sides were slain that all the battleground was turned red with their blood. This made the Great Spirit so angry that he turned the battleground into red stone, and to this day it is the most sacred Indian ground in America. For countless generations many Indian tribes have made their pilgrimages here to obtain the unusual and sacred red pipestone from which they made their pipes of peace.

Lone Eagle then journeyed north to Lake Traverse, which had been the early home of Antone Renville, where he met a band of Sisseton Sioux. This small band is known as the "Si-si-ton-wans" in the Dakota language, meaning Swamp Villagers. From here he visited the "Ti-ton-wan" (Teton), Dwellers-on-the-Prairie, on the Cheyenne River. After visiting the "I-hank-ton-wans" (Yanktons), Village-at-the-End, and the "Ma-wa-ta-dan," or Mandans, he traveled west to the home of "Ho-he" (Assiniboine) Sioux, on the Poplar River, in Montana.

With a family of the Assiniboine he then went to the Crow Reservation to visit the Custer battlefield, on the Little Big Horn. Here he met a number of Sioux whom he had known while with Chief Big Elk's band. Several of the braves had married Crow girls and were now living on the Crow Reservation. Here he again met White Fawn, his childhood playmate, whom he had not seen for ten years. Her stepfather, Two Bears, was a Crow rancher and owned large herds of cattle and ponies.

Lone Eagle was welcomed as one of the family and was employed as a cowboy with other Indians to look after the stock. Most of the cattle and ponies on the reservation belonged to the Crows as a tribe and bore the brand "I D" (Indian Department). The few that were owned by individuals mostly belonged to squaw men and mixed bloods.

Chapter III

The Old Corral

IN 1908, TWENTY YEARS AFTER MY PARENTS LEFT ME WITH MY aunt and uncle in New Jersey, I had grown to manhood and, having just received my diploma from college, was making plans to start in some kind of business for myself.

My aunt and uncle had talked but little of my parents, and I remember of often asking them why my father and mother did not write. Tears would fill their eyes, but no explanation could be given. As the years passed no letters were received, innumerable inquiries had proven futile, and I was told that probably my parents had died somewhere in the West.

My aunt and uncle had always expressed the wish that I enter a professional career of some kind near them in New Jersey. This I, of course, considered, but my chief thought and desire was to go west, so within a few weeks after my graduation I bade farewell to my relatives and friends and was on my way. I made the trip quite leisurely, spending several days visiting many of the large cities of the Middle West.

I decided to see the Yukon Pacific Exposition and so went to Seattle, Washington. I spent several days viewing the interesting sights and, having never seen an Indian in his native costume, I visited the Indian Village, where many families represented several Indian tribes. While watching one of the tribal dances, a tall, well-featured Indian boy, who had been standing on the opposite side of the circle from me, came over and, in a friendly manner and with a broad smile, said in very good English, "How, Lone Eagle, when did you come here?" To say that I was surprised and puzzled was indeed putting it mildly. He, seeing my great surprise and wonderment said, "Why, Lone Eagle, you sure no forget me, I am Walking Bear, at Pine Ridge School." I was positive now that he had mistaken me for someone else. I told him my name and that I had just come from the East. He seemed greatly surprised and vexed and after looking at me closely for a moment, turned and walked away. Occasionally he would glance at me from where he stood watching the dance.

After spending two weeks at the fair, I went to Council Bluffs, Iowa, where I worked in the Great Western department store for a little over a year. I had accumulated a little money and decided to visit the Dakota Black Hills. Many times, since my visit to the Exposition, I had amusingly thought of the Indian boy who had mistaken me for an Indian friend of his.

While at Council Bluffs I made the acquaintance of a stockman named James LaForge, who owned the Diamond Bar W Ranch, in Washington County, South Dakota. He had often invited me to visit him, and I wrote that I would be happy to accept his invitation. He met me at Gordon, Nebraska, where we were to drive overland, some sixty-five miles north, to his ranch.

Gordon was then a small frontier town built along the railroad, typical of the prairie cities whose chief industry was to supply the neighboring cattle ranches and Indian reservations. It consisted of one long street with the usual hitching racks on either side. Strung along this dusty street were a little one-room post office, a saddle and harness shop, a blacksmith shop, livery barn, barber shop, and three or four general stores, which furnished the neighboring ranches with anything from a ton of dried apples to rolls of barbed wire or blackstrap molasses by the jug or barrel. It was not unusual to have some rancher drive up in front of one of these general stores with three or four six-horse freight teams and spend an entire day loading up a year's supplies for his ranch, located perhaps fifty to seventy-five miles away. Such a trip would take him and his wagon drivers from three days to a week. He thought nothing of giving the store owner a two-to-three-thousand-dollar check on a bank in Chicago or Sioux City, where he was in the habit of shipping a trainload of range beef each fall, and it also was not unusual to see the cowboy or rancher count out a thousand or two thousand dollars in gold or greenbacks from a belt around his waist or from a leather sack carried in the tool box under the front dash, locked only with a harness snap.

The rest of the main street consisted of a couple of saloons, a Chinese laundry, eating places, and the customary wooden-front hotels. The price of the average hotel room, with no keys, was about a silver dollar. Keys were never heard of in the West in those days. The only thing that would be likely to interfere with your night's sleep would be the noisy bar-room across the street or some over-indulging cowboy who might bang on your door with the butt of his Colt six-shooter inquiring if you knew what room he had paid for sometime earlier in the evening.

At six you arose with the guests and, in the hallway down stairs, you patiently awaited your turn for the tin wash basin, and dipping it in the rain barrel close by, you took one quick look for wiggle-tailed tadpoles, and then you washed up for the day. The eleven-foot roller towel behind the door also was serviceable for all guests, and when two yards of it would stand unsupported in the corner you hunted up the desk clerk, who was bartender next door also, and received a new circular piece of linen which reminded you of fourteen-ounce canvas. The particular one I located that morning had about the same flexibility as a threshing-machine belt.

It was a far cry from what I had been accustomed to in my New Jersey home but it was also to be the beginning of a most eventful and unusual chain of circumstances in my life, beyond my wildest dreams.

My rancher friend arrived in town about noon with a six-horse freight outfit consisting of a triple-box Studebaker wagon and trailer. He drove up alongside the loading platform of one of the general stores and, leaving the wagons, put his team in the livery stable down the street.

I watched with much interest while he arranged the loading of his wagons. Two clerks trucked sacks of flour, case after case of canned goods, boxes, and barrels out to the platform, while Jim carefully packed them in his wagon. Not less than three tons were packed in the front wagon and at least two tons in the trailer. A few articles procured from the harness shop and depot warehouse completed the list and we were ready for our long drive to the ranch.

We left Gordon early the next morning, the first rays of the sun finding us well on our way. The sunrise on the vast prairies is extremely colorful and beautiful. I was all excitement. The early morning air was cool, crisp, and exhilarating as we sat high on our wagon seat. Jim drove the sturdy six-horse team with apparently no more effort than was his easy, pleasant conversation. The stillness was broken only by the creaking of our heavily laden wagons and the steady tattoo of the horses' hoofs on the sun-dried road.

The prairie road ahead seemed to extend as far as the eye could see and then fade out on the distant horizon. Only occasionally did we come to a coulee or wide draw, when it was necessary for Jim to use the brakes. If the dip was not too steep or long he would take a running start down the incline and up the other side. But, when the road was winding or more abrupt, he would slow up the first wagon with the iron foot brake, which made a loud scraping noise as the wooden shoe was forced heavily against the two rear iron tires. The trailer brakes were controlled by a long rope attached to the end of a pole with the lower end fitted into the upright brake standard.

We saw many small herds of pronghorns feeding in the early morning. They would raise their heads for a moment as we passed and then continue their feeding. An occasional long-eared jack rabbit would go limping along on three legs. I, at first, thought the rabbit was crippled and wanted Jim to stop and let me try to catch it. I was informed that this three-legged hop was only a habit of these animals and that all four of those long legs would be put into immediate action should the need for more speed arise.

An occasional covey of grouse or sage hens would suddenly fly out from a bunch of sagebrush alongside the road, and our horses would make a sudden swerve clear out of the road, only to hear a word from the driver and all would be well again. Jim said that only a comparatively few years before, countless herds of buffalo roamed these same prairies. Even then, as we rode along, I saw many old whitened buffalo skulls, with their black stubby horns, lying over the prairies.

All this was most interesting and romantic to me. The sun now was slowly beginning to drop toward the west, and Jim informed me that we would soon reach the Nebraska state line and would cross over into South Dakota, which also would be the south boundary of the Pine Ridge Indian Reservation.

We traveled until late that evening and made our camp on a small branch of Wounded Knee Creek. We pulled up to a little clump of cottonwoods a few rods from the side of the road and proceeded to unhitch the horses. The harness was removed and placed on the ground beside the wagon, after which the horses were led down to a water hole in the otherwise dry creek bed. Apparently the creek was dry at this time of the year except for scattered water holes in the low places.

Six nose bags were partly filled with oats and hung on the horses' heads, and then each horse was hobbled by buckling a pair of leather hobbles on the front feet. When they were through eating they were relieved of their nose bags and permitted to graze along the coulee.

The Western freight and wagon teams are accustomed to being hobbled, and move about carefully by taking short hobble-chain-length steps with the front feet, or raising both feet together and crow-hopping along in a sort of leapfrog movement. However, they seldom stray far from camp during their grazing.

Jim chopped some sagebrush and greasewood and started a small fire. When it burned down to a bed of coals he put on the coffee in a tin pail, a pan of baking powder biscuits, and a skillet of bacon and eggs. After opening up a can of tomatoes and of corn, we sat down on the wagon tongue and enjoyed a meal that would tempt any hungry traveler. A few uninvited ashes from the fire settling on my tin plate did not discourage me in the least.

When our evening meal was finished and the tin dishes washed in the creek, Jim climbed up on the lead wagon and threw down the bedroll. Untying it, he showed me how to roll out a cowboy's sleeping equipment, which we arranged on the ground near the wagon. The cowboy's bedroll is as much a part of his everyday equipment as his boots and heavy stock saddle. The rancher, freighter, or mule skinner always carries his bedroll when he travels a day's journey from his ranch house. He knows that he is always welcome to a meal or night's lodging at any ranch house or cow camp, but just as often he finds himself miles from the nearest ranch when night overtakes him.

This universal Western bedroll consists of a tarpaulin cover of waterproof, eighteen- or twenty-ounce canvas some fourteen to fifteen feet long and half as wide. This is spread on the ground and on one half of it is spread a number of the old, well-known, four-point Hudson Bay blankets and a couple of good, wool-filled Western sougans. Over this is pulled the other half of the tarp, which is held in place by snaps and rings along the two sides. Using his saddle or war-bag for a pillow, the traveler spends the night warm, dry, and comfortable in any weather.

When Jim had completed the arrangement of his bed we rolled in and I spent my first night out on the quiet prairie under the ever brilliant Western stars. The quietness really startled me. Only the steady munching of the horses eating grass and an occasional jingle of their hobble chains could be heard.

Suddenly, a lone coyote broke the stillness by that never-to-be-forgotten wail. His quick, sharp bark gives you the feeling that at least half a dozen must be just over the knoll behind you, then another faint yap-yapping tells you that, far in the distance, his call was heard. I looked around but saw only a couple of our horses grazing peacefully on the low hill. I could hear Jim's slow, deep breathing so knew that all was well. I soon fell asleep, and, all too soon, I was awakened by a cheery "Hello" and the information that we would be rolling at "early-sun-up." I was up and ready to help him bring in the horses. I also succeeded in harnessing two of the gentlest horses while Jim harnessed the other four.

Our breakfast over, I watched as he carefully packed up our bedroll by folding both edges to the middle of the tarpaulin-covered bed and then rolling it tightly from head to foot, making a neat roll about three feet long by eighteen inches in diameter. After tying it with a rope he boosted it upon top of the wagon. A bed thus rolled could remain in the wagon or on the ground in an all-day rain without even getting the blankets damp.

A last look around and we were again headed north. We seemed to have the rolling prairies all to ourselves until about mid-morning, when we saw an object moving on the road ahead. We soon discovered it to be another freight outfit coming toward us. While yet some distance away, Jim recognized the outfit as belonging to a neighbor, some thirty miles beyond his ranch. As the empty wagons drew up alongside, they stopped and we chatted with the occupants for at least half an hour. They also were on their way to the railroad at Gordon for supplies.

These observing ranchers and cowboys knew everyone within a hundred miles by the brands on their stock and always referred to them as their neighbors. Their conversation concerned the various conditions on the range, weather, stock prices, and the general happenings among the ranchers' families since their last meeting. Again, a few miles farther on, we saw several riders to our left trailing a small bunch of cattle. Two of them were leading pack horses loaded with what I took to be their beds and grub supplies. They left the small herd and rode over to see us with a hearty "Hello Jim, howdy Stranger," and after a few exchanges of local news, we were again on our way. We saw no one again until about noon.

As we rounded a bend in the creek, we came into full view of a large group of Indian tepees. Jim immediately recognized it as Chief Big Elk's camp of Sioux. He told me he was personally acquainted with the friendly old chief and many of his band, and that we would camp with the Indians for the noon meal.

I had never seen an Indian camp before, and was pleased at the thought of being in a real Indian village, in their native surroundings. Jim talked with several of the men while I stood close by observing the lodges and inhabitants. A score or more dogs kept up a continuous barking until quieted by half a dozen stones which were hurled at them by some of the men.

We went to see Chief Big Elk, who lived in the large tepee near the center of the group. As we neared the tepee, several dogs announced our coming by their fierce barking. Jim stooped and walked in ahead of me. The old chief, who was sitting on the ground opposite the door, nodded with the words "How, Mita Kola" (Hello, My Friend) and motioned him to sit down. The chief evidently did not notice me until after he had shaken hands with Jim, then after extending the customary greeting to me, he motioned us both to a seat on a pile of blankets.

Our host talked at some length with my friend, punctuating his conversation with many graceful gestures of the Indian sign language. From time to time during his conversation, the chief would turn and look intently at me; finally, pausing to address me directly, he said that I reminded him very much of someone by the name of Lone Eagle, who had lived among his people for many years as a boy. I explained my identity and told him of the Indian boy at the Exposition. I also told him of my parents and their supposed death somewhere in the Dakotas. I asked who this Indian boy, Lone Eagle, was and what of our resemblance. The old chief told me that Lone Eagle was not an Indian, but a white boy whom he had adopted and raised after the death of the boy's parents, the white missionaries.

I became interested and asked more about Lone Eagle and his parents. After a somewhat prolonged pause he again began to tell, a few words at a time, the story of the coming of the Black Robe missionaries to his people, their work among them, the birth of the white papoose, and the winter camp in the Black Hills. I sat in silent wonder as I listened to his strange, romantic story.

Could these white people have been my mother and father? Truly, my parents had come to the Dakota territory in 1888, the same year the chief described the first visit of the missionaries to the band of Oglalas when they were camped on White River. Although I could not distinctly remember my parents, I recalled their photographs, which I had seen many times in my aunt's family album. I knew that my father was tall and of slight build, and my mother was shorter and of stouter build — the exact description given of these missionaries by the chief.

I could scarcely believe this story of the two white people from the country toward the early sun and how near their description was to that of my own parents. Could this white boy, whom the Indians called Lone Eagle, be my own brother, a brother whom I had never seen or even known was in existence? If not, why then had I been mistaken for him? All my thoughts seemed to center on this story of the white boy. After some inquiries, I was told that Lone Eagle was living with a brother-in-law of Big Elk on the Little Big Horn River, in Montana.

By this time I had full intentions of going to the Crow Reservation just as soon as I completed my visit to the Diamond Bar W Ranch. We continued our driving and during the rest of the trip I could think of nothing else.

Along in the late afternoon we arrived at the ranch. It was certainly a most ideal and picturesque setting. The low-built and spacious ranch house was nestled in a grove of cotton-woods in the bend of the river, the rustic sun porch running the full length of the house. The cowboys' bunkhouse extended some distance east of the main building connected by a long, flower-covered trellis. The wagon house, blacksmith shop, corrals, and large red barn were located some one hundred yards away, down near the river.

We drove up in front of the warehouse and unhitched our team, and a couple of the boys, who had been working around the corrals, came up and took the horses to the barn.

Upon entering the house I was introduced to Mrs. LaForge and their daughter, Juanita, a charming and graceful girl of about nineteen. With her dark eyes and black hair she made a striking picture dressed in her white broadcloth shirt, blue jeans, and a pair of tan cowboy boots. Bob, a younger brother of fourteen, was nursing a sprained ankle from being thrown by a yearling calf a couple of days before.

Although far removed from a railroad and the convention-alities of a modern town, their home had all the appearances and conveniences of any city residence. Pictures and paintings on the walls, draperies, hanging kerosene lamps in glass beaded chandelier, and colorful rugs created a colorful atmos-phere. The great stone fireplace, massive leather chairs, shelves of books, and the general air of hospitality all lent a feeling of restfulness and comfort in every part of the house.

Supper, announced by a bell in the cupola over the kitchen, brought the six cowboys from the corral. Two of the boys proved to be younger brothers of Mrs. LaForge, from Minne-sota. Curley Hickman, an old-time cowboy from Montana, who was known on the range as "Dad," always said that when he was six years old his father threw him up on the back of a half-wild mustang while on a drive from Texas to Montana and told him to stay there and ride, or walk the rest of the way to Montana. That was forty-four years ago and he had been riding ever since. Tom Smith was perhaps forty and a little on the heavy side, as most cowboys go, and answered to the name of "Arizona." When referring to his home state he always called it "Airy-zo-nee." "Tex" was at least six-feet four in his stocking feet, and with his boots on was a towering giant. He was born in the Big Bend country and claimed relationship to Sam Houston. He had ridden the range in most of the southwest states and trailed up from Texas with a herd of longhorns from the X I T outfit in the late eighties, and stayed to work on the northern ranges. When Tex opened up conversation concerning his Southern exploits and drives across the old cattle trails, "Arizona" always chimed in, good naturedly, by adding that Tex couldn't have returned to Texas if he'd wanted to, as he had once forgotten to return an X I T horse when he suddenly left the outfit one dark and stormy night. Tex always claimed he got lost and couldn't find his way back to camp anyway.

The one cowboy native to the Dakotas was Jack Red Owl, full-blood Sioux Indian and champion roper of the ranch. Jack always spent his spare time in the evenings drawing pen-and-ink sketches of cowboy and Indian life. All these cowboys were top hands and a finer and more loyal bunch of men could not be found in all the West.

I had always heard that the Western cowboys had the age-old habit of treating the Eastern tenderfoot to a real introduction of ranch life by inducing him to mount some apparently sleepy-eyed plow horse, which generally turned out to be a cyclone on four feet.

My knowledge of horsemanship consisted of a couple of summers spent on the dairy farm of one of my cousins in northern New Jersey, and when I was invited to go out with a couple of the boys to drive in a bunch of cattle one day I, naturally, was somewhat suspicious of the buckskin-colored broncho they had picked out for me. I wondered just what they had rigged up for me, or more likely, for their own entertainment, and whether I would come out second best at the finish. However, the boys were most considerate of my situation and showed me every assistance and respect.

Tom was the Beau Brummell of the ranch. His riding equipment was a show exhibit of which any saddlery shop would be proud. His snow-white Stetson set him back at least $45 and was adorned with an inch-wide band of diamondback rattler's skin. His shirt and neckerchief were of turkey-red silk. The hand-carved, two-inch leather belt atop his Levis was a maze of silver-star conchas and a massive buckle of solid Mexican silver inlaid with a golden steer's head.

A pair of heavy, silver-mounted spurs were buckled onto his well-polished, handmade, Justin high-heeled boots. His .45 Colt six-shooter, belt, and holster also were heavily mounted in silver and ivory. His flower-carved, Miles City saddle was a single-rig, centerfire job mounted with silver cantle nameplate and several pounds of Mexican conchas. His horsehair bridle and roller-spade bit were adorned with the same material. His outfit would loom up in a blaze of glory at half a mile on the prairie, but no one ever said Tom could not ride and rope with the best of them.

Tex and "Dad" Hickman were from the old school and knew the trails and cattle business as experienced by but few of the still-active cowboys. Both men had ridden on the long spring drives from Texas to Montana and the Dakotas when the vast herds of longhorns were still being moved north.

Jack had come to the ranch only a few years before, after his graduation from Carlisle. He was one of the best corral and all-around trick ropers I ever knew, either on or off a horse.

Bob and Juanita were raised in the saddle and knew the ranch business as well as their father. Juanita and I took many rides together over the ranch, and I found her a most charming companion; she could converse on many subjects of travel and world events.

Mrs. LaForge had come out to the Dakotas as a schoolteacher some thirty years before and had married the handsome cowboy who rode for the Diamond Bar W. Jim had the habit of stopping at the little country schoolhouse every time he had occasion to pass, just to get a cool drink from the well in the schoolyard.

Mrs. LaForge confidentially told me that there was a much better spring of water not over half a mile down the road but she never let on she knew about it. Jim used to stop there years before the school was ever built but he never mentioned that to her either. Also, Jim was about the thirstiest cowboy in that part of the country after the pretty young schoolteacher arrived from Minnesota, but when school was out and she returned to her home for the summer, Jim came only as far as the old spring when he was thirsty, and not nearly as often. However, she admitted she was glad when her school term began again, because the handsome cowboy had promised to bring along an extra saddle horse and take her to some of the neighborhood dances that were given when any of the ranchers put up a new house or barn.

Not too long after her return, Jim decided to build a new house of his own on his newly acquired ranch. She apparently liked the new house and its lone bachelor, because the next fall saw a new teacher in the little prairie schoolhouse and the neighboring cowboys for miles around got all dressed up for a grand wedding at the Diamond Bar W Ranch.

James LaForge was a grandson of an early-day fur trader on the northern Minnesota frontier. Jim came to the Dakotas in his early twenties and his first job was riding for the famous "Scotty" Phillips buffalo ranch near old Fort Pierre, eventually coming to the Diamond Bar W Ranch, which he bought out some years later. He proved to be a successful stockman and, at the time of my visit, was branding some fourteen hundred calves on the spring roundup.

After my brief visit at the ranch I bade them adieu and started for the Crow Reservation in Montana in search of Lone Eagle, whom I now fully believed to be my brother.

I reached the Crow Agency and inquired as to the whereabouts of the Sioux chief's brother-in-law, Two Bears, and learned that he lived on his ranch on the Little Big Horn a few

miles from the agency. I borrowed an Indian's pony and saddle, and in a few hours' ride was within sight of the log ranch
buildings. As I rode up to the small group of buildings, I saw,
near a large corral, several men and boys branding some colts.
I rode up and watched them at their work. Four of them were
mounted and doing the roping; five were engaged in keeping
up the fire and handling the hot branding irons. All four of
the men on horses and two on the ground were Indians and
wore their hair in long braids, otherwise, they wore boots,
spurs, and black, broad-brimmed hats like the white cowboys.
The other three were in similar dress, but wore their hair
short.

As they worked around the fire, heating and passing the hot
branding irons to the stocky Indian who applied them to the
helpless animals, I noticed that one of them was of fair complexion and his hair was not black like the rest. As I sat watching him, he picked up a stick to stir the fire. The slender
sapling was too long to handle easily so he pulled a knife from
his pocket and began cutting the stick in two with his left
hand. My mother also was left-handed. After stirring up the
scattered bed of coals he came over to the side of the corral
nearest me and stood watching some colts in an adjoining
enclosure.

I looked at him closely for some time. Surely, he did possess
a marked resemblance to people I had seen before. Was this
the white Indian boy for whom I had several times been mistaken? Yes, I could now plainly see, he really did have a noticeable similarity to me. He seemed the very likeness of the
photo I had often seen of my mother. Was my hope really to
come true? Could he really be my brother, the son of my own
parents, whom I had come so far to see?

I dismounted from my saddle and walking up to him asked,
"Are you Lone Eagle?"

"Yes," he said in a somewhat surprised tone.

"Are you the son of the white missionaries of the Sioux?"
I continued.

"Yes, I have been told so by the Sioux. Why do you ask?"

"Then you are the son of my own father and mother. You are my brother." I shall never forget my joyous feeling and the expression on his face, as I told him the story of our parents.

Here we were, brothers, sons of the same parents, one born and raised in the center of cultured New Jersey society; the other born in an Indian tepee and brought up an Indian, in the heart of the warlike Sioux Nation.

We were, after that, an inseparable pair. I told him of the country toward the rising sun, and he, in his broken English, told me of his life among the Sioux.

I stayed with my brother on Two Bears' ranch until the following year, and we talked much of our plans of taking up a ranch of our own somewhere in Montana as soon as the coming Sun Dance and tribal buffalo hunt were over.

Chapter IV

The Buffalo Hunt

THE CROW INDIANS, KNOWN AS THE "KAN-GI-WI-CA-SA" AMONG the Sioux, own the largest private herd of buffalo in the state of Montana, numbering some twelve hundred head, which range between Pryor Creek and the foothills of the Pryor mountain range on the reservation.

It is their custom to hold a buffalo hunt every fall about the last of August or the first part of September. This early date is selected because of the method of caring for the large quantities of meat in the ancient custom of all plains tribes.

The tribal council is called together and, after taking into consideration the condition of the range grass and the fatness of the herd, they arrange the date for the hunt. Also, mounted scouts are sent out to find the exact location of the roving herds. A few days before the hunt, all the selected hunters set up their camp near the location of the main herd.

The Crows are a friendly tribe and are among the wealthiest in the West, in land and native-raised food. Their 2,800,000 acres of fertile rolling prairie and mountains give them ample feed for wild game and their thousands of fine whiteface cattle. In recent years it has been the custom of the Crows to extend invitations to all of the dozen or more tribes in the neighboring states to come and be their guests at the Buffalo Dance and buffalo feast following the great hunt.

The venerable old war chief, Plenty Coups, and his council send Crow messengers to the chiefs of the various tribes to invite representatives to the dance and feast. It so happened that Two Bears was selected as messenger to invite Chief Two Moons, of the "Sha-hi-ye-na" (Northern Cheyennes), whose reservation is on the Tongue River, just east of the Crow country. Two Bears said that Lone Eagle and I could accompany him to Lame Deer, a two-day journey on horseback. Two Bears was then over sixty years old and was one of the finest horsemen among the Crows.

As we rode over the rolling prairies toward Lame Deer Agency, Two Bears related many interesting tales of the various parts of the country we traversed, once a famous buffalo hunting ground of many of the western plains tribes. He pointed out a deep canyon at the lower end of a flat stretch of bench land where he, as a boy, saw his people drive large herds of buffalo down across the flats and over the cliff, after which the hunters had only to go down below the sixty-foot cliff and find tons of buffalo carcasses.

After reaching the agency we rode on to Two Moons' ranch and were welcomed by the old chief and his family. This was my first meeting with this old warrior chief of Custer Battle fame. It was he who led the Cheyennes against General Custer on that memorable day on the Little Big Horn, in 1876.

Our mission over, we returned to the Crow Reservation in time for the buffalo hunt. Lone Eagle and I had been invited to participate, and both were filled with excitement over the coming event. Lone Eagle already had accompanied them twice and had been successful in killing four of the buffalo with his Winchester carbine from the back of his fleet Indian pony.

The hunters had selected their campsite at the foot of the Pryor Mountains, about four miles from the old buffalo salt lick. Counting Two Bears, Lone Eagle, and myself, there were thirty-four Crow hunters in the camp. Among the older men were Chief Plenty Coups, Old Curley (only survivor of Custer scout fame), Harry White Man, Sidney Black Hair, Pretty On Top, White Man Runs Him, Louis Lyon Shows, Max Big Man, and a very old squaw man by the name of Thomas LaFarge. However, most of the hunters were younger men, in their twenties and thirties.

They were all typical of the Plains Crow Indians, tall, swarthy, their black hair in long braids, with many of the younger men wearing high-crown, black cowboy hats, with beaded bands and eagle feathers tied to the band. Some wore chaps, spurs, and high-heel boots, cowboy fashion. Others wore only moccasins on their feet.

Every man was mounted on his best and fastest horse. All had heavy-calibre rifles except four or five old men, who carried Indian bows with steel-pointed arrows.

These old men with the bows and arrows were going to ride their ponies into the herd and shoot buffalo as they did years ago when buffalo roamed the same hills in vast thousands, and they depended on their skill for meat and clothing.

Each year the young Crows honor a number of these old veteran buffalo hunters to ride first into the herd, mounted bareback or with Indian saddles, using a war bridle of rawhide rope tied around the pony's lower jaw, and armed only with bow and arrows.

Four of these old men were to participate this early August morning and we all watched with eagerness to see them ride into the herd for the run. They rode along behind the long, low ridge until they came opposite the feeding herd. We followed, at least three hundred yards behind the four riders. Then as they rode up to the brow of the ridge to where they came into view of the nearest of the herd, they quickened their pace in the direction of the herd and rode as close as possible until the buffalo scented danger and began to walk slowly away. One of the men rode almost into the herd before they became aware of him. He rode up alongside a big bull and shot an arrow into his shoulder at less than thirty yards. When the herd began to run, the riders each selected an animal and followed him as close as possible. When he saw he could overtake his buffalo, the rider would swerve out and ride up along-side and shoot his arrow into the buffalo just back of the front shoulder, or any spot likely to down him.

Each of the four hunters succeeded in killing his buffalo with arrows. One old bull ran for at least two miles before he finally fell to his knees and tumbled over with nine arrows sticking from his side. Sidney Black Hair killed his buffalo with two arrows, the second one lodging in the buffalo's heart. Max Big Man accomplished a feat that day that I have never forgotten. One of his arrows hit a young buffalo cow just back of the third rib and came out between the fourth and fifth ribs on the opposite side, nearly half of the arrow showing on the opposite side. I was so amazed at this feat of strength that Big Man gave me the arrow and it is still one of my prized possessions. The arrow is twenty-eight inches long, grooved, has three guide feathers, and the steel arrowhead is made from a four-inch jackknife blade.

Sidney Black Hair is still living on the Crow reservation as this story is being written, but Max Big Man died in 1951.

When the old men had each killed a buffalo, the other hunters, with rifles, used about the same procedure, only scat-tering out over the hillside for several miles in order not to be in line of fire of the other riflemen. The many riders strung out along the various small bunches and picking out their quarry, rode into the most advantageous position and downed their buffalo.

Sometimes the hunt became quite exciting as some wounded buffalo turned on his pursuer and, with head lowered, made a rush that no horse or rider cared to meet. Many narrow es-capes are experienced in these hunts, as an enraged bull can become a ton of untamed fury in a second's notice.

One rider's horse stepped into a prairie-dog hole and turned a complete somersault, throwing his rider into a headlong heap right alongside of a wounded buffalo cow. Indian and buffalo saw each other at about the same time. The buffalo struggled to get up, just as the dazed Crow boy was trying to pick up his rifle. Horse, buffalo, rider, and carbine were all in a tangled heap. The buffalo half rose to its knees, staggered a few feet, and fell dead across the Indian's gun. When a couple of the boys saw the accident, they came to the rescue, only to find a dead buffalo, a horse with a broken front leg, one broken rifle, and a badly scared Indian, but this same boy got another horse and succeeded in killing seven buffalo before the hunt ended that eventful day.

Lone Eagle had three buffalo to his credit and I had killed one. The total for the hunt that day was 176. These carcasses were loaded on wagons by means of teams and rope tackle. We also loaded several of the wagons by backing up to the buffalo and pulling them up a pole incline by means of our saddle horses and lariats. Some of the meat was distributed direct from the hunting grounds to Indian families living in the vicinity of Pryor. The rest of the meat was taken to the Crow Agency in some twenty to twenty-five wagons and distributed to each family who wished to come for it.

August and September are warm and dry in Montana, and the sun shines clear and bright. Each Indian family prepares its buffalo meat by cutting it into half-inch slices. They then dip it into dry salt or brine and hang it up in the sun to dry. This process of sun drying takes about three to five weeks and the meat is known as jerked meat or "jerky," and will keep for months or years. Similar to cured or dried beef, it is hung up anywhere, away from prowling dogs or wild animals. The salt brine dipping prevents flies or insects from bothering it.

After these buffalo hunts, this sliced meat can be seen hanging from lines, trees, or specially built racks, in every camp or dooryard. It can be eaten months later, boiled, fried, stewed, or just plain raw. I have eaten hundreds of pounds of sun-dried buffalo jerky prepared in this way by the Indians and know of no better meat.

As soon as the buffalo meat arrived at the agency camp, five entire carcasses were carefully cleaned and prepared for the feast. They were placed in pits and barbecued by several experienced members of the tribe. The process takes about twenty-four hours.

By the appointed day of the Crow buffalo feast, hundreds of wagons came, from every direction, bringing entire families from every part of the reservation. Teams were unhitched, camp equipment unloaded, the tepees were set up by the womenfolks, and soon the great circle of gaily painted tepees made a most impressive sight.

Visitors from many neighboring tribes set up their tents and tepees among the various bands. There were Cheyennes from the Tongue River, Flatheads, Blackfeet, and Assiniboines from the north, Umatillas from Oregon, several Bannocks and Nez Perce from Idaho, Shoshones from Wyoming, and many Sioux from the Dakotas. Not many years ago these same tribes met only on the warpath. Now they smoke the pipe of peace and are welcome visitors.

About noon, the camp crier announced that the buffalo feast was ready. The five barbecued buffalo were taken from the pits and six thousand pounds of steaming-hot, delicious meat was ready for the waiting hungry men, women, and children. Five long tables were set up and Crow men at each table gave each visitor a paper plate containing two slices of bread, cold potato salad, pickles, cabbage slaw, and coffee. At the other end of each table, the five lines of Crows and their guests were given as much of the steaming hot meat as they desired.

This serving of the buffalo feast presented a colorful affair. Some were in gaily beaded buckskin costumes, others in colored shirts, neckerchiefs, store clothes, and plain ranch attire. Women wore bright blankets, and an occasional one had a dusky papoose strapped to her back. Laughing children ran in and out among the crowd, eagerly awaiting their share of the feast.

The meat was completely consumed by seven thousand hungry Indians and a sprinkling of white visitors from the neighboring ranches and towns.

The feast over, the ceremonial dancing began and lasted all night and long into the next day. The steady, rhythmic beating of the tom-toms and chanting of the dancers and singers during the night was something ever to be remembered. Our camp was near the dancing pavilion and when not watching the dancers, we lay awake and listened to the steady Indian music.

The next day we spent most of our time going among the Indian lodges visiting the families from the various tribes. Several of the Sioux from the Dakotas were camped in a group among the visitors. Lone Eagle took me to their camp hoping that perhaps there might be some one he knew from Pine Ridge. While he was busy going from lodge to lodge inquiring for any of his boyhood friends, I noticed a very elderly Sioux sitting among some Blackfeet, conversing in the sign language. I leisurely walked over to where they were and, receiving a nod of welcome from one of the men, I sat down among them.

I had often watched Lone Eagle and the Crow men talk in this language of the plains, was always fascinated by it, and wanted to see and learn something of this graceful silent language as used by the Indians. Just as soon as I had seated myself, the elderly Sioux picked up a beautifully beaded elk-skin pouch and took from it a long red stone peace pipe. He filled it with kin-ni-kin-nik tobacco and, after lighting it, took a few puffs and passed it among the group as a sign of friendship. When it came around to me, I took a few puffs in recognition of their friendship and was amazed at the great beauty and fine workmanship of the pipe. I looked at it long and carefully before I passed it on to the old warrior next to me. Then and there I decided I should like to become its owner. After watching these venerable sign talkers for a while, I joined Lone Eagle in a tepee among some of his former friends.

I mentioned the incident of the beautiful peace pipe and expressed my great desire to negotiate its purchase. Knowing that the elderly Sioux could not speak English, I wanted my brother to talk to him in his own language and arrange for the purchase of the pipe. We hunted him up and Lone Eagle told him of my desire to obtain the treasured pipe. Black Thunder, in his stoic manner, did not seem to be much interested in disposing of his pipe.

"My brother will give you maza-ska wik-che-mna (ten silver dollars) for the pipe." A silent shake of his head was the only answer.

"Maza-ska wik-che-mna ake zap-tan (ten, again five silver dollars)," continued Lone Eagle. A longer silence—but still a shake of the head was our only answer.

Lone Eagle looked at me for my consent for a higher offer.

"Maza-ska wik-che-mna, nom-pa ake zap-tan (ten, two times, and again five, silver dollars)," was offered the old Indian, as I counted out twenty-five silver dollars in my hand. Black Thunder took one glance at the stack of silver dollars in my outstretched hand, and, replacing the pipe in his beaded pouch at his belt, turned on his moccasined heel and, in perfect English, grinned and said, "No soap, son."

Chapter V

Homesteading in Montana

THE BUFFALO HUNT AND BARBECUE BEING OVER, THE GREAT circle of Indian lodges were taken down, as the Crows and their visitors returned to their various homes. The hundreds of tepee poles were carefully stacked upright against large trees to keep them until the next encampment. These long, slender lodge poles were brought down from the foothills for the use of visitors who lived at too great a distance to bring tepee poles of their own. Those living nearby dragged their sets of tepee poles behind the wagons, or used the old conventional plains travois and carried their tepee covers, children, and equipment behind their saddle ponies. Only a few tepees remained standing when we left the village for Two Bears' ranch.

Lone Eagle and I were now going north in search of a ranch of our own. Two Bears had told us of some likely locations up on the Missouri and in the Musselshell River country, where he had hunted buffalo as a young man. He remembered the snow was never too deep in the sheltered brakes, and the buffalo grass was good the year round. My brother had two branded Crow horses, Grey Eagle and Gypsy, part Arabian and Morgan stock, which were equally good as saddle horses or pack animals. I also had two Crow ponies, a calico and a buckskin, named Lariat and Comanche, respectively.

Lariat was about the best all-around cow and rope horse on the reservation. In the corral or on the roundup, he could just about turn on the proverbial dime, but he never quite got used to the idea of submitting humbly to a pack outfit. Several times, while on long trips, I had carefully arranged my pack and bedroll on him and no sooner had I started merrily on my way, when this calico-hued paint job would lower his head, let out a lusty bawl, and proceed to scatter my belongings all over the surrounding landscape.

Comanche, however, was not quite so good on the rope, but under a pack would follow carefully along all day behind my saddle horse and never loosen a rope.

It was now the third of September, and we were taking our leave of Two Bears. White Fawn, his niece, was to take the train from Billings the following Monday for her junior year at the Carlisle Indian School. She was very fond of Lone Eagle in her typical shy Indian manner, and it was not at all unnoticeable that he was beginning to realize that she was now growing out of that — "just a little girl member of the family" — as he had always looked upon her in the past.

September is a beautiful month in Montana. The browning prairie and brilliant hues of the high mountain ranges in the distant haze of the morning sunrise gave us the ever-awed feeling of its vastness. Mountain peaks a hundred miles away seemed only a little distance beyond the next hill. We were, seemingly, lost in the great expanse and magnitude.

We headed our ponies north and, after hours of rolling and fenceless prairies, we could see in the distance the familiar landmark known as Pompey's Pillar. This natural rock formation rises some two hundred feet out of the surrounding valley and was used in former days as a signal tower for warring tribes. Lewis and Clark saw it a century and a half ago and Captain Clark carved his name and the date (1806) some one hundred feet up on its north wall. This inscription is plainly visible to this day. The formation was named after Sacagawea's young son, whom Captain Clark had given the nickname of "Little Pomp." Beautiful moss agates and native sapphires are found quite plentifully in this area. We also encountered several rattlesnakes among the rocks at the base of the pillar.

We crossed the beautiful Yellowstone River at this point and camped for the night. The next day we headed for the Bull Mountains, riding over mile after mile of rolling prairie, where thousands of range cattle were seen feeding on the grassy hills. We made our camp that night high up on the south slope of the Bull Mountains, where we found a good spring. Near by was a sheep wagon but we saw no one around. A coyote pelt was hanging from a pole in front of the wagon, and a set of harness was thrown across the wagon tongue, the front end of which was resting on top of the neck yoke.

The next morning, we again continued over the mountains and soon found ourselves descending the north side into the Musselshell River country. The country here was rolling and covered with rich buffalo grass. The range stock looked sleek and fat. We met and talked with several cowboys who were riding for the "7 9" outfit, which had a large horse ranch near Sand Springs, in old Dawson County.

In the distance we could see a long, thin fringe of cottonwoods and knew we were nearing the Musselshell River. Just before we rode into the little valley town of Roundup, we saw in front of us some strange looking windows and doors carved out of the seeming solid rock wall or cliff just ahead, and were more surprised as we rode nearer to see several persons looking at us through these windows, and smoke issuing from several chimneys. The ancient-appearing cliff dwellings actually were occupied by families who were working in the coal mines close by. These rooms are cut out of the solid rock cliff and, by building a few yards of wall in strategic places, the dwellers had succeeded in building several comfortable homes. So far as I know, they are the only real native cliff dwellers in Montana.

We spent the night in the bustling little cow town of Roundup and then began a two days' ride up the Musselshell River, toward the Crazy Mountains. About noon of the second day we ran into a small bunch of range cattle as we crossed a shallow place in the river, and not far from the crossing, we saw one of the cows stuck, belly deep, in a mudhole. The code of the open range is to help any person or animal in distress. So Lone Eagle and I took down our lariats and threw loops over her horns, and, tying to our saddle horns, we picked good footing for our ponies and tightened the ropes. After a half hour of pulling, resting, and maneuvering around we finally succeeded in pulling the cow out on solid ground, but were careful to keep her down until we got our ropes off her horns.

Exhausted for the moment, she refused to get up, so I tried to assist her by grabbing her horns and twisting her head in an upright position. After resting for a few minutes, she gave one big bellow and made a mad lunge at me, and kept right on coming, while I made a wild scramble over a couple of boulders and climbed into my saddle just in time to save the slack in my Levis. That is what I call gratitude — even from a cow — but they will do it every time.

We rode up the Musselshell River to Harlowton and decided to camp for the night. After supper, we strolled up town and dropped into the Graves Hotel to inquire about some land locations. There, we were fortunate in meeting Cris Graves, owner of the new stone hostelry. We overheard him telling a couple of cowboys about a small herd of cattle that had strayed away from their usual feeding grounds somewhere along the river. I heard him say that his brand was a quarter circle over Y9.

I remembered the unappreciative cow we had pulled out of the mudhole and recalled it bore a Y9 brand and so informed the old gentleman. He did not seem to think this was the same bunch he was looking for, but from his description of the herd, we were quite certain they were the cattle he wanted. He said he would give a dollar a head if they were delivered at his corrals at the edge of town.

Lone Eagle and I talked it over and decided to bring the bunch to the designated place. We retraced our ride of the day before and, about sundown, we drove through town with the fifty-two head of Y9 beef. Fortunately, they were the bunch

Graves was looking for, and as soon as we had them safely inside the corrals he gave us a check for $52, as promised.

The next morning, we went over to the bank to cash our check and when looking it over again we noted that the old gentleman had not signed the check, but had scrawled Y9 in the place where his name should be. We called the teller's attention to the omission of a signature, but he only smiled and counted out $52 without any hesitation and casually remarked that Mr. Graves could neither read nor write, and that his signed brand was worth a king's ransom in more than one bank in the state.

From Harlowton we decided to look over the Judith Basin country to the north. We passed between the Little Belt Mountains to the west and the Big Snowy Range to our right. Between these beautiful mountain ranges is a pass known as Judith Gap. After passing the Gap we came into the southern end of the Judith Basin. Here we began to see wheat fields, and, as we rode nearer Lewistown, the fields were more frequent and larger until, finally, we rode along grain fields comprising hundreds and thousands of acres. Great stacks of grain could be seen all around us, waiting for the threshing crews, and several machines were threshing from the shocks in huge unfenced fields. Grain farming was being carried on here on a larger scale than I had ever seen. The Judith Basin country had been taken up by homestead settlers a few years before and was now being developed into one of the great wheat-producing areas of the West.

Approaching Lewistown from the west we came to the brow of a hill and, suddenly appearing below us, was this picturesque little city, nestled in the valley along Spring Creek. Before us loomed the magnificent and azure-hued Judith Mountains, apparently just beyond Spring Creek, so clear is the atmosphere at this four-thousand-foot elevation, but it is a day's journey even to the nearest foothills. It is indeed a most picturesque and enchanting view.

Lewistown was a bustling little city of some seven thousand population, supplying the large farms and ranches for more than half a hundred miles around. Here, great ranches of central Montana obtain their ranch supplies over distances greater than the total length and breadth of some New England states.

We rode down the street and passed the Dark Horse livery stables. From the many saddle horses, teams, and freight wagons around the old barn we concluded there must be a horse sale in progress but were informed that a meeting of the Montana Stockmen's Association was being held at the old Day House, a famous meeting place of local stockmen.

Since my brother and I were interested in the possibilities of ranching in Montana, we thought it worth our while to attend some of the gatherings and meet some of the local citizens and ranchers. We received several invitations to attend their meetings and found the ranchers very friendly and hospitable, as is universal with all cattle communities of the West.

Among the men we met for the first time that day and whose friendship lasted throughout their lifetimes, were the venerable Thomas Cruse, owner of the famous N Bar Ranch, near Grass Range; Granville Stuart, discoverer of gold on Gold Creek, in 1868; "Teddy Blue" Abbott, of Giltedge, son-in-law of Stuart; David Hilger, state historian; Roy Ayers, who later became governor of Montana; and Walter Winnett, who owned the "O5" Ranch, where the county seat of Petroleum County now stands. Old Chief Rocky Boy, of the Rocky Boy Cree Indian tribe, and Charlie Russell, Montana's famous cowboy artist, were also two of the popular Lewistown visitors.

After several days in this picturesque county seat of Fergus County, we continued our journey east across the Judith Mountains. Just as we were passing the old mine tunnels, we saw a long string team slowly coming up the winding road ahead. As it drew nearer, we noted it was not the usual string of horse- or mule-teams of the freighter, but was seven yoke of oxen and six heavy wagons loaded with wheat. These oxen were owned and driven by an elderly man named McDonald, who had a ranch up in the Judith Mountains. Ox teams were getting to be somewhat of a rarity in Montana even then, and to see seven yoke and six wagons in one long string, driven only by a single jerk line was a rare sight indeed. Remembering the long steep winding hill we had just come up before meeting the oxen, we were not a little curious as to how the driver would make this mile-long, steep, down-grade with his heavy wagons and long string of steers, so we rode back to the top of the hill to watch.

To the driver, however, it was all in the day's drive. He pulled up to the top of the hill and, without even a word to his oxen, he set the heavy iron foot brake and, untying a rope and tackle began taking up the slack in a ninety-foot rope that reached to the long pole in the brake standard of the last wagon. Each wagon brake pole was attached to this main brake line and by the pulley attachment on his lead wagon he managed the speed of the five rear wagons. Thus, perfectly controlled, this 150-foot train descended the long winding hill with ease. No doubt many of the older residents of central Fergus County will recall this last of the old Montana bullwhackers.

After descending the Judith Mountains, we rode along the McDonald Creek bottom lands toward Grass Range. Looking north, Black Butte, one of the best known landmarks in central Montana could be seen. This unusual mountain rises majestically several thousand feet out of the surrounding low plains, like a huge pinnacle of black rock, and is plainly visible for fifty miles. Even in winter, when snow covers all the surrounding country, this lone butte rears its black head practically bare of snow.

Stopping in Grass Range we met several cowboys from the N Bar Ranch, who told us of some good ranch land that was open for homesteading some forty or fifty miles east of there, between the Winnett Ranch and the Musselshell River, with plenty of open range for stock raising.

Grass Range was then a village of some dozen or more houses, one general store, and post office. Mail service was twice a week by stage from Lewistown, some thirty-five miles across the mountains. Wagon freight outfits supplied the one general store. The genial postmaster was notary public, justice of the peace, constable, real estate agent, insurance writer, and homestead locator on week days, and Sunday School superintendent on Sunday. He gave us considerable information about the country bordering the Musselshell River.

While spending the night at the old Teigen Ranch, on McDonald Creek, we met a cowboy who was driving some cattle down to the Musselshell River. He was on his way home and said he would be glad to have us ride with him in that direction, and would tell us about the country in general, as he had ridden most of the range between here and the river. The cowboy had planned to drive a small bunch of cattle as far as the Winnett Ranch but, as the day had been warm, we traveled slowly and decided to camp for the night at a small ranch a few miles this side of the O5 corrals. Our friend said he knew the rancher and that it would be all right to put up for the night. I have conveniently forgotten the rancher's name, but he and his family gave us a most cordial welcome to make ourselves at home. We sat down to a hearty meal and truly enjoyed the evening with the rancher, his wife, and seven little tow-headed spalpeens. During the evening meal, there was never a dull moment and never more than four of these little demons crawling on or under the table at any one time. We could almost hear each other talking when an occasional lull occurred. The oldest boy, age eleven, swatted his sister in the eye with a meat platter following an argument over a piece of meat, and general bedlam ensued. All in all, it was a most lively evening meal.

As the evening wore on, and conversation lagged, we were taken to the one large bedroom at the end of the sprawling log house, and, since our host insisted it was not necessary that we bring in our own bedrolls, we occupied the sleeping quarters in the house. The lamp had not been out more than thirty minutes, when someone let out a lusty "ouch," stating that a pin was somewhere in the blankets. In the dark we could not locate the cause of our annoyance, so it was forgotten and all turned to sleep again. However, more stickers were in evidence, and we concluded that the blankets must be full of sand or prairie thistles. Again, we rolled over and tried to sleep. I'm sure I had fallen asleep, when suddenly I was awakened by a series of muffled shots somewhere in the room. Half awake, half asleep, I finally became aware of someone kneeling on a blanket in the center of the floor, holding a lighted match, and while I was trying to awaken myself enough to realize what was going on, I heard a loud "wham! bang!" on the floor again, as I recognized our friend in scant attire softly counting "13-fourteen-15," as he brought his boot down on the blanket with his other hand. Our blanket "sand" turned out to have legs and plenty of bite. Sleep there was impossible so we quietly gathered up our clothes and spent the rest of the night in our own beds out in the old corral. From that night, ever after, we always laughingly referred to this place as the "buggy shed."

While at the Winnett Ranch, where the county seat of Petroleum County now stands, a group of French-and-Indian cowboys told us of several new homesteaders who were camped in the Cat Creek Basin, about fifteen miles northeast of the ranch. On further inquiry, we learned of a trail which would lead us to these basin settlers.

During this four-hour ride over the rolling sagebrush land we never saw a sign of a house or man. Several herds of cattle and horses were passed and a number of pronghorns and coyotes were seen in the distance, but there was no mark of civilization — nothing but the wild, lonesome prairie stretching as far as the eye could see. At last we rode up to a sage-covered hill and suddenly before us loomed a beautiful stretch of valley land — the seeming paradise of the home seeker.

Here, in the valley below, we saw our first signs of settlers since leaving the ranch. We counted three partly constructed log cabins and a tent. Heading for the nearest cabin we found three young fellows; two were industriously throwing mud into the crevices of the logs, while the other smoothed it down with a trowel. When noon came we were invited to sit down on a log on the dirt floor and eat a much relished meal of beans, bacon, and soda biscuits.

During the next few days, we rode over all this valley country for miles around, selecting a suitable site for our ranch. Before the setting of the sun on the fourth day, we had picked out a location with shelter for our buildings and stock, where good water and ample range for our stock would be available during all seasons of the year. Thus was the beginning of our new ranch home in central Montana.

As this part of Uncle Sam's public domain was in its virgin state and still unsurveyed, it was necessary for us to run a survey from some known point to our new claims in order to get the exact number of the section for filing our squatters' rights. From survey maps obtained in Lewistown we hunted up the nearest old township stakes, some twelve miles west. With the aid of a homemade compass and three hundred feet of baling wire, we ran lines to our claims, established our section, range, and township location on our map, and returned to Lewistown, where we filed our declarations to locate a squatter's right on our respective 320-acre ranch homesteads. These applications we filed on the tenth day of October, 1910, from which date our established residence began.

After completing our crude survey and establishing our ranch boundaries we borrowed a team and wagon from the Winnett Ranch and began cutting and hauling pine logs from the Badlands, some six miles to the north, and started construction of a log ranch house on our claims. Such materials as windows, flooring, roofing, and dimension lumber were necessarily hauled from Lewistown, seventy-five miles away, requiring from four to six days to cross the mountains.

Wishing to put up livable quarters before the winter set in, we hired an experienced French-and-Indian wood cutter and completed one of the rooms to live in, while we worked on the remaining five as weather permitted. Since the size of the rooms depended only on the length of logs we cut, we made all our rooms of ample dimensions, eighteen feet wide by twenty-two feet in length. A large, stone, frontier-design fireplace in the living room and den was one of our chief attractions.

Except for the three new homesteaders down the valley, our nearest neighbors were at the Winnett Ranch, some fifteen miles southwest, and the Ashley Ranch, about the same distance northwest. The beautiful valley surrounding our ranch was about eight miles long by five miles wide, containing approximately twenty-five thousand acres. On the north, it emerges into the Badlands, while on the east, south, and west are found the more broken or rolling prairies. Our free open range then extended north to the Missouri River, a good forty-five miles, and several miles to the south, east, and west, giving us a free open grazing range of over eight hundred square miles or some five hundred thousand acres.

Our first winter was spent mostly in putting up our buildings, when the weather permitted, and although there were many below-zero days and nights that winter, we also had plenty of bright, sunny days when we could work on our ranch buildings.

The following spring and summer saw several new homestead settlers in our midst, taking up land some four or five miles above us on Cat Creek. They spent the summer and fall building and putting up necessary improvements on their various claims. By late fall, most of our newcomers had completed their cabins and were secure to enjoy a few months of leisure, until spring would come with its seasonable ranch activities.

During the summer, my uncle and aunt had shipped numerous boxes and trunks of my personal belongings from the East. Our ranch house was now beginning to take on the appearance of a real home. I divided everything with my brother, Lone Eagle, who never had possessed or even seen any of the heirlooms of our own parents. We were very proud of our library of eight hundred handsome leather-bound books, once the private library of our parents. There were many early photographs of our parents and relatives, numerous old family heirlooms, and boxes of old personal effects and souvenirs.

Our maternal grandfather had once been postmaster at Morristown, New Jersey, before the Civil War and had accumulated one of the largest collections of United States coins and postage stamps of his day. This collection was expressed to us in two ancient Wells-Fargo strong boxes and was quite the center of attention for our many visitors, when we displayed it in large glass picture frames on our den and living room walls, along with a large collection of Sioux and Crow Indian craft accumulated by Lone Eagle from the various reservations he had visited. Our entire library was always at the disposal of any of our friends and neighbors who wished to make use of it.

It would take too long to describe in detail the experiences of our first winters spent in this vast expanse of Montana plains. We visited each other much; often the entire group would gather at one place and spend the day. For pastime, we played games, told stories, read books, listened to "canned" music, and made many articles of cowboy equipment and ornaments from hammered silver, braided leather, and colored horsehair. Several of our group wrote first-hand stories of Western adventure for magazines and the home papers back East. We worked on necessary buildings and ranch improvements when weather permitted. We often furnished our tables with a variety of fresh venison, elk, and pronghorn, after a successful hunt in the Badlands. It was a welcome variation from our daily rations of beef, bacon, sage hens, and long-eared jack rabbits.

We were neighborly by circumstance as well as from choice. If one person ran out of something his neighbors were always willing to share with him, and this was no rare occurrence, as our nearest store was forty-five miles away. I remember of one of our neighbors making a trip of ninety miles on horseback, in a snowstorm, after fifty pounds of groceries for himself and a neighbor. Our nearest post office was at Weede, fifteen miles east of us on the Musselshell River. The mail was brought to Weede by stage from Melstone, some forty-five miles south. It arrived twice a week during the summer and once a week, or as often as possible, during the winter. I remember, once, of being on a homeward trip from a ranch near the stage road, about halfway between Melstone and Weede, when a raging blizzard came up very suddenly about noon, and I decided to ride for the nearest shelter.

I was not too familiar with that part of the country at the time and calculated the nearest place of refuge for myself and saddle horse would be along the river. As I rode down to the river, I saw an old abandoned log barn just ahead, and figured it wise to stop for shelter. When I swung open the door I was not a little surprised to see the mail stage driver and his team inside. His stage had got stuck in a snowdrift some distance down the river and both horses were down. His only chance was to unhitch the team and return to the old barn. He had tied one sack of the mail on one of the horses and two horse blankets on the other and then hurried to safety — none too soon. The stage driver, my saddle pony, and I occupied one stall and his team of horses the other. We placed one horse blanket on the ground and the other one over us, using the mail sack for a pillow, and shivered through that long February night without even removing our boots. The next day, we returned to the buried stage and dug two more mail sacks out of the drifted snow. The mail did not go through that day, but it sure was no fault of the driver.

The spring of the year was also a difficult time to get our mail through on schedule. The Musselshell is often a raging torrent for weeks after the first spring thaw.

The old post office at Weede consisted of a few handmade boxes in one corner of Mrs. Weede's kitchen. When we made our thirty-mile round trip after our mail, it was not at all unusual for the kindly old lady to invite us to dinner with the family before she hunted out our mail for us.

More than once in the spring, when the river was out of its banks, we would come to the bank on the opposite side from the office and cut loose a couple shots with our six-shooters in order to attract their attention, and they would come out and ask us whose mail we wanted, as it was customary to get the mail for any rancher or homesteader living near our route of travel, or who would come to our ranch after it. If we thought the river too high or swift to ford or swim our saddle horses, they would put the mail in a flour or grain sack, tie a small stone in one end, for weight, and then throw it across some narrow place. So far as I know, not a single sack was ever lost. We always took turns carrying the Basin mail on horseback. In summer, we received our mail about once a week, in winter from one to two times a month. Once I remember we received no mail for over two months.

On one occasion, we ran out of kerosene at our house and during our conversation with a neighbor, when we had stopped to deliver his mail, we mentioned being out of oil for our lamps. The kindly neighbor, although possessing but one gallon of oil himself, generously shared equally with us. When this supply was exhausted, Lone Eagle and I spent our evenings in total darkness for five weeks, our only light being the radiance from our cookstove. The only calendar in the valley

LONE EAGLE, EAGLE BAR RANCH, MONTANA (PHOTO TAKEN 1911)

was possessed by a neighbor, but one day I marked out a calendar for three months on a cracker box lid. I afterwards found out that even a calendar will not tell the day of the month. I nailed our homemade calendar on the door and each morning, for nearly three weeks, I marked off a day. One bright Sunday it came my turn to make the trip after the mail, and after reaching the ranch house I casually passed some remark about this being a fine Sunday. The lady at the window informed me this was not Sunday but Friday, so I returned home from the office on Friday, two days before I started. I had kept my calendar correctly, but started it two days late.

On another occasion, when we neglected to get a calendar on our fall trip to Lewistown, we devised a calendar of our own, from September to March, and nailed it to the kitchen door, which was the customary place for all household information. However, Lone Eagle and I could not agree which months had thirty days and which had thirty-one, so we compromised by making them all thirty days and then added three extra days for March and it came out all right.

More than once we were welcome guests at the several homes where womenfolks ruled the kitchen, instead of the bachelor biscuit dust mixers, as was the case at our house. This always was a treat we have never forgotten. Cooking at our cabin was much varied as to style, but the "makings" always remained about the same; beans, biscuits, and meat for breakfast; biscuits, meat, and beans for dinner; and more meat, more beans, and some biscuits for supper. One day, however, I borrowed a package of mincemeat and, while my brother was away, I chopped it all up fine and enclosed it in a crust made of flour, lard, and boiling water. As I had no pie pan I baked it in the frying pan. When Lone Eagle came home for supper, I proudly showed him my skill in the culinary art. He worked on it with his knife for a while and finally pried open the crust and ate the contents. In the morning I found my pie crust nailed to the door and in bold letters he had written: "Sole leather for sale here."

As the warm spring days came we again resumed our ranch

improvements. We took much pride in the ranch and had now completed most of our buildings, corrals, a large storage cave, and several miles of good fence. We were now eager to plow up a quarter section or so of prairie sod and sow some small grain and alfalfa for our stock. We had purchased a couple of heavy draft teams from the Winnett Ranch, and a wagon and some farm machinery. Lone Eagle and I had accepted a job on the N Bar Ranch for the annual spring and fall roundups in order to acquire some stock of our own. We had bargained with the ranch to take most of our pay in spring calves at $12 per head and we were to receive $55 per month each.

We occasionally saw families in covered wagons driving through our valley in search of homesteads on Uncle Sam's public domain. Those families who were living on surveyed lands were known as "homesteaders" or "honyonkers"; however, if they settled on land not yet surveyed, they were generally referred to as "nesters" or "squatters." Any newcomer was a "scissorbill" or more commonly known as a "tenderfoot."

Along with our honest and industrious newcomers we also received a few of the lawless and so-called bad men. These outcasts drifted in from all parts of the East and West. They soon came to know each other and, in a short time, began to take advantage of the distance from enforced law and proved a menace to the country in general. The situation became worse, until several secret meetings were held among early settlers, and word was sent to our nearest county seat, some seventy-five miles away. On receiving no reply, a delegation was sent to have the law enforced in our neighborhood.

The county officials were unwilling to send officers so great a distance into an unknown country, so, on returning, we decided on a few laws of our own and organized a group of vigilantes, made up of some sixteen ranchers and homesteaders. Immediately after the next depredation by this outlaw gang, our entire troop visited their rendezvous and gave them just three days to leave the country or the "3-7-77"* fate

* Vigilante term meaning "three feet wide, seven feet long, and seventy-seven inches deep.

would be theirs. Before the dawn of the next day their cabins were empty. Only one of this group ever returned to our neighborhood and it was upon oath that he would live in peace with his neighbors. His promise never was broken.

Several more of this class invaded our territory at various times and tried to operate their favorite game of fighting off peaceable claim squatters, stealing, and often rustling and driving off the homesteaders' livestock. The selected vigilantes soon discouraged men of this brand from working in our territory. The rustlers often quarreled among themselves and, on several occasions, after the smoke had cleared away we found one less to bother us.

The last of our lawless customers was a man from the Eastern states who had won a notable reputation as an all-around bad man and fighter. He arrived in our midst late one fall, in a rather quarrelsome mood, boasting at some length of his self-evaluated importance to our community. He appropriated a choice claim in the heart of our valley which previously had been selected by a former settler, who, at the time, was away working for his winter's grubstake. As squatters' rights then consisted of possession by the best man, he informed the entire settlement of his intention of doing as he pleased with this claim and any of the settlers who crossed his path.

His case was discussed by our committee, but before we had come to any decision, he had visited the cabin of one of our first three pioneer settlers to demonstrate his skill as a pugilist. While he was explaining how many men he had already put out of business, our peace-loving neighbor produced a Colt six-shooter from his bunk and proceeded to show his skill as a ranger. Two bullets took effect, and by the help of a passing neighbor, he was taken to the home of the Basin missionary who administered flour-sack bandages and peroxide for four days until the nearest doctor arrived from some seventy-five miles away. By the time our desperado had partly recovered from his wounds, he thought it best to depart from our immediate neighborhood. Peace and happiness reigned in our valley from that time on.

As new settlers moved into the valley, it became apparent that we would have to establish a school for the half dozen or more children in our community. In the fall of 1912, we called a meeting and petitioned for a school, as we were seventy-five miles from our county educational department and the nearest school. School districts had, as yet, never been organized in unsurveyed territory, but our county educational office agreed to supply a teacher provided we supplied our own schoolhouse. The valley settlers agreed to this and soon erected a suitable log building. Each homesteader and rancher was assigned to furnish a certain part of the building. Some put in the rock foundation; others cut and hauled logs from the Badlands; still others purchased windows and doors or furnished and laid the flooring. Our particular assignment was to supply the shingles, while a couple of our neighbors helped us put them on. The seats were handmade from pine lumber. The stove was an improvised steel barrel with one end chiseled out for a door. It stood on a foundation of rock slabs imbedded in adobe. The blackboard was made of flooring, painted black, and hung on the front log wall. This community-built school building was soon completed, and in the following month instruction began.

As most of the children came to school on horseback, the school yard was always filled with saddle horses staked out on long lariats. On snowy or rainy days, the saddles, saddle blankets and bridles were piled on the floor in the back of the schoolroom. Wraps and books were placed on a long bench on one side of the room.

It was not at all uncommon for some of the older boys to carry a Winchester on their saddles, as jack rabbits and pronghorns were often seen along the way to and from school. During one of our most severe winters, when the snow lay deep for many months, a twelve-year-old boy and his younger sister were followed by a pack of five timber wolves for over an hour and, when they came too close, the boy dismounted from his saddle pony and succeeded in shooting two of the pack, less than one hundred feet behind them.

Early in May of the following year, an aunt and uncle from southwestern Iowa came out to spend the summer at the ranch. My uncle, who was a retired minister, was a welcome addition to our valley community. He organized the first valley Sunday School and held services every two weeks in our log school building. Cowboys, ranchers, and homesteaders came from miles around to attend these services. The cowboys always called him "The Sky Pilot," and the name stuck so well that many a family in central Montana knew the elderly minister only as "The Sky Pilot of the Musselshell." Many an old-time cowboy, rancher and early day buffalo hunter who had not darkened the door of a church in forty years came to hear the venerable old minister.

The winter of 1913 was one of the coldest we had witnessed. The thermometer often went to forty and forty-five degrees below zero and snow was so deep in places that the fences were completely buried for weeks at a time.

One incident still will be remembered by many of the early valley settlers. In March of 1913, one of our first settlers died. Modern burial facilities were not available in our community, so we improvised as best we could. One of the neighboring homesteaders had a plank horse trough about twelve feet long and two feet wide, so we sawed this trough in two and boarded up one end, making a coffin six feet long and two feet wide. One of the settler's wives put some straw in the bottom and lined it with a bed sheet. We had no black paint, so I scraped a tin cup of soot from our fireplace and mixed it with kerosene. With a handful of turkey feathers, I painted the box black.

We knew of no relatives at the time, so we decided to bury the remains on a hill not far from his cabin. As the winter had been long and cold, we dug through solid frozen ground for several feet. Our Sky Pilot was away for the winter, and none of us was sure what sort of services would be appropriate. We all wanted to do the best we knew how for our respected friend and neighbor, so we sang several songs and my brother concluded the service by reading some verses from the Bible.

It was not until several years later that a brother came into our part of the country making inquiry for our deceased neighbor. We accompanied the visitor to the hill above the cabin, in search of his brother's grave, but were never able to locate it again.

Cowboys and settlers enjoy an occasional get-together and often ride long distances to a party or dance given in what they call their local neighborhood. When any rancher built a new barn or house, it was customary to give a house-warming dance. It was not at all unusual for the cowboys' and ranchers' families to ride twenty to thirty miles to attend one of these old-time square dances. About dusk, the half-a-hundred guests would begin to arrive on horseback and in straw-filled bobsleds. Everybody would be there from "grandmaw" to the smallest youngster, and everybody joined in the fun.

I well recall one of these old time dances given at the Eagle Bar Ranch one Christmas just after we had completed another one-room addition to our log ranch house. By eight o'clock "Big Ed" Fleury began to tune up his old violin. Harry Smith worked awhile on his battered guitar, while the Valley "schoolmarm" tuned them in on the (somewhat out of tune) piano. When they finally announced the first dance number, every rancher and cowboy who had "brung his own gal" were out on the floor.

There were some good dancers, and some not so good, including a few, like myself, who were even worse, but everybody danced just the same. The boys outnumbered the girls several to one. The cowboys waited their turn along the wall, but a girl who sat out more than one dance in an evening was a rarity indeed, "grandmaw" included. The square dance was the most popular among young and old and the less you knew about its many calls the more fun for the rest. Big Ed could call square dance numbers all night and never do the same one twice over.

About midnight, the host brought around well-filled, homemade sandwiches and coffee. The very small and younger children were put to bed in a room by themselves. They were bundled up and laid on the beds, cots, and floor during the dance. The babies were so numerous that it was no easy matter to wade in among the youngsters on the floor to reach the ones farthest from the door. It was quite a regular occurrence for some mother in the middle of a dance to recognize the lusty cry of her youngest, and excuse herself from her dancing partner of the moment, rush into the bedroom, and proceed to nurse her hungry offspring. As soon as the little fellow was carefully tucked in on the floor and sleeping again, the mother would return to the scene of gaiety and resume her dance with her waiting partner. If the dance should end and another one begin while the mother was away, it was customary for the lady to have the next dance with the same partner. How the mothers could tell their own children from the two dozen or so bundles on the floor and beds was always a mystery to me.

These gala events always lasted until the grey streaks of dawn began to creep over the eastern horizon, when the sleepy fiddler would announce that "Home Sweet Home" would be the next number.

It was the custom for everyone to put on their full going-home clothes for the last dance. Girls put on their heavy wraps, cowboys buckled on their chaps and spurs, hunted up their heavy sheepskin mackinaws and ten-gallon Stetsons, and threw open all the doors and windows as they danced the old familiar number. It was an amusing sight to see a roomful of colorfully costumed men and women going through a fast square dance to the tune of the old fiddle and jangling spurs. Many a dashing cowhand landed unromantically on the corn-meal waxed floor as his spurs tangled with his own or someone else's boots.

As soon as the last strains of music died away, the men went out to get the saddle ponies and teams ready, while the women proceeded to gather up their precious bundles of family pride in the crowded bedroom. Soon all were wending their way out across the prairies to their several homes, after an evening long to be remembered.

Travel was slow over the trackless and fenceless prairies, and driving had to be done with caution. Snow often filled the coulees and ravines level with the surrounding plain and what few roads there were between the ranches were often completely obliterated by the drifted snow. Therefore, it was necessary to pick out the ridges and most likely looking stretches of prairie.

The rancher always had certain buttes, ridges, or landmarks as guides from one place to another when snow covered the roads. Hence, travelers going long distances found it necessary to make the trip during the daylight hours.

Chapter VI

Roundup Days

IT IS THE CUSTOM IN THE WESTERN CATTLE COUNTRY FOR THE ranchers to hold a roundup every spring and fall. The spring roundup usually starts around the middle of May and lasts some six weeks or so, two or more ranch outfits working together on overlapping ranges. Where large ranches graze their stock over large areas, it is customary to send one or more cowboys as representatives to work with neighboring roundups. They are known as "Reps." Each cowboy generally uses a string of from seven to fourteen horses during the roundup. The boys put in long hours in the saddle and, as it is not practical to carry grain for their horses, one or two horses are used each day in the week, in order to have a fresh horse for each day's strenuous work. These outfits consist of a dozen or more cow punchers, a day horse wrangler, and a cook. The chuck wagon is always driven by the cook.

Our chuck wagon was a regular ranch kitchen on wheels. A large pantry was built in the rear of the wagon and when the end door was let down, everything was there for the cook, from baking soda to imported spices, and the door formed a large table where he prepared his tempting meals. The familiar water barrel was always to be found strapped to the side of the great wagon, and an ample supply of the best canned goods was carried in the wagon. During the day, the wagon also was piled high with the cowboys' bedrolls and war-bags of personal effects.

On these great roundups, we had the best the land afforded. The coffee would float a horseshoe, and we would butcher the fattest yearling steer on the range. In the daytime, we wrapped the meat up in a heavy canvas and laid it on the ground to keep it cool. At night, we hung it up on poles to keep the coyotes and wolves from getting it. At the first streak of dawn, the cook would do a Comanche war whoop and we would all roll out, roll up our bed and tarps, and hit for the mess tent.

After breakfast some would help the cook with the dishes while others caught and harnessed the horses, four for each wagon. Tents were torn down, the bed and chuck wagons loaded, our saddle horses caught, and we were ready for work.

After the roundup foreman or "wagon boss" laid out the range to be worked that day, the cowboys would scatter out in a systematic order so that the country would be thoroughly combed, driving all the cattle toward the wagon. Enroute to the wagon, the moving cattle were known as a drive, and all drives combined were called the roundup. At chuck time, two or more men were left to hold the roundup herd, while the rest would ride to the wagon. After dinner they changed horses and returned to work the roundup.

The cows and unbranded calves were cut out, with the beef steers cut out separately. After the calves were branded, we returned to camp for a little rest. Each man had his turn at night herding, usually for two hours. The night guards usually were sent out in pairs, depending somewhat on the size of the herd to be held. As each two-hour period ended, one of the riders would come in quietly and wake the next two who were to stand guard, and so on until daylight, when all would be up and ready for the next day's drive.

When working very rough land, like the Missouri River brakes and Badlands, it was impractical to take wagons, so we would make up a pack outfit on one of our extra horses and make trips into the canyon country in small groups. We would build small Indian fires of cottonwood and sagebrush and when they had burned down to embers we would roast our beef over the hot coals, on the end of a forked stick. Anyone who has never eaten beef roasted in real Indian fashion, has missed something.

Our fall roundups often consisted of from one thousand to two thousand head of four-year-olds, which were the shippers' favorite beeves of forty years ago.

BRANDING IN THE OLD CORRAL

The roundup had its fascination and dangers for all hands. Occasionally at night, when the cattle are bedded down, some sudden noise or movement among the herd will startle them, and in a matter of seconds they are on their feet and start a wild stampede. They may start in any direction, and anyone in the path of such a wild running herd is unfortunate indeed, as hundreds of clashing horns and thundering hoofs can easily spell doom. If a horse should stumble and leave its rider afoot, his chances of survival are slim.

While trailing a beef herd to the railroad we made from ten

to twelve miles a day. They usually trailed out in long strings, some steer always being the self-appointed leader. I recall one of these roundup drives when we were driving some sixteen hundred head from the brakes on Crooked Creek, in northeastern Fergus County, to Melstone, some sixty miles south. We had been on the drive for six days, slowly trailing south along the west side of the Musselshell; the weather had been hot and dry for October, and we could hardly see the herd for the thick alkali dust. The boys on the drag were wearing their silk neckerchiefs over their faces to keep out part of the dust, which burned their eyes and throats.

We finally came in sight of the stockyards and loading chutes, just out of town along the railroad, and were heading our lead steers into the corral wing, when along came the express flier and let out a couple blasts for a railroad crossing. Before the echo rebounded from the nearest hills, every animal in that herd had started on a mad stampede. When the dust finally cleared away, not one was in sight of the yards, and it took us half a day to coax that bunch of dogies up to those pens again, and we had to make the last mile drive between trains.

Winter feeding in Montana was a rare occurrence. This Montana bunch grass or "buffalo grass" cures on the stalk and is equally as good in March as it was in August.

An amusing incident on this particular drive may still be remembered by some of the H Cross boys from the lower Musselshell. One of our cowboys had met the Sand Coulee school teacher at a river dance, and decided it might be in his favor to stop in for a visit at the ranch home where she roomed and boarded. So he brought along an extra boiled shirt and got a shave and haircut for the occasion. When we made our camp at Sand Coulee on our return trip, without a word to any of us, he took off about dark to see the teacher, some two hours' ride away. It was clouding over fast when he left, and looked as though it would be a dark night, so he left a lighted lantern in his tent to guide him on his return, as there were no trails between our camp and his evening's destination. Soon after his departure, it began to rain quite hard, and the night was as black as the proverbial stack of black cats. So, about the time our swain should be returning to camp, some of the boys slipped over to his tent and blew out the lantern. We all stayed awake and waited for his return, and about 5:30 A. M. a pretty mad and rain-soaked cowboy arrived. He had been riding up and down the river most of the long, dark night, looking for his guiding prairie light.

At the ranch and on the roundup, many horses are ridden for the first time and often cause a great deal of sport. The Western broncho has the well-known habit of bucking when first being broken to saddle and some retain this habit always. Changing horses is often an exciting occasion, especially to the rider who picks a bad one for the first time.

One day on our ranch, we rounded up a bunch of pretty snaky-looking bronchos, none of which had ever been ridden. Some of the riders proposed that each of the boys ride one of these green bronchos to break the monotony of the past week. All heartily agreed to this proposal — although I should have preferred to be a looker-on. Of course, that would not have been good ranch etiquette under the circumstances, so I joined in with the rest. As luck would have it, I was first on deck. The boys helped me saddle my horse, and, getting a firm hold of the rope reins and hackamore cheek, I connected with the horn and swung into the saddle. He immediately bucked, in a small circle at first, and I had no particular trouble keeping my seat without pulling leather. He finally made a break and ran a short distance, then suddenly stopped short, and again started to buck. This time I lost one of my stirrups and had the pleasure of leaving my seat a foot or more skyward, managing to come down just as the saddle came up. This soon got monotonous and I was pulling leather at a great rate. I succeeded in getting my balance about the time he stopped to get his breath. My ride would never have made entrance fees among the rest of the boys, but I was satisfied with being allowed to get out of the saddle — unassisted by my mount — rather than being removed spread-eagle fashion.

My brother was considered a good rider, even among good cowboys, and also had his chance to demonstrate his skill in the saddle. He had some trouble in getting in the middle of his bay mustang, but, once seated, the fun commenced, and the joke was on the broncho. We watched the waltzing pair while he fanned her over the head with his Stetson and busted a couple of holes in the air with his six-shooter. This was very entertaining, but the best stunt of the day was pulled off by Joe De Yong — a Blackfeet Indian boy. Joe was a good buster, but his broncho was a little the better of the two. When the cayuse was roped out of the herd we sized him up as a bad one. We had some difficulty in getting the saddle on him and, even after this was accomplished, he tried to pitch it off. Joe was standing at the long end of the rope eyeing his pitching adversary when the foreman yelled, "Say, Joe, the boys will make up ten dollars if you ride him without a hackamore." Joe was game, so the headpiece was removed. The horse was blindfolded and Joe hopped into the saddle. Then the blindfold was taken off and the show was on. The bronc gave several snorts, ran a ways, stopped short, and began things in earnest. Joe grabbed all the saddle leather he could find and held on like a leach. True to his race, he wore a grim face and said nothing. The broncho, not accomplishing his purpose, stopped, snorted a few times, then started bucking in a small circle. After completing a few of these, he made a bolt in a straight line for perhaps a quarter of a mile, when suddenly he gave two or three parachute leaps. Then Joe gave one and landed on his head and shoulders in a patch of cactus and let out a yell that would have done credit to a dozen of his race. Joe was badly used up, but no bones were broken. He got his ten dollars and another ten besides, but the entire bunch could not throw in enough to induce Joe to do that stunt over again. The broncho remained on our ranch for many years but was never saddled again. We named the outlaw "Flying Joe."

The cowboy, as a rule, is always willing to wager a few dollars on any kind of a game of chance, especially so if there is a horse in it. I learned my lesson in gambling rather early in life, and I, long since, have lost all interest in anything pertaining to a game of chance. It was in 1911, when my brother and I made our first trip to Miles City with a group of Indian cowboys driving a herd of some two hundred horses to the stockyards of the well-known Clark Brothers annual horse sales. We arrived in Miles City the latter part of September, after a hundred-mile drive from the Wolf Mountains and Little Big Horn country. Many thousands of horses from all over the state were brought in and sold, later to be shipped to all parts of the East.

The streets were lined with hundreds of stockmen, cowboys, and Indians from every range from Powder River to the Rockies. Buyers were there from every state as well as army representatives from several foreign countries.

The Al. Furstnow and Cogshell saddlery stores were general meeting places. It was there that I first met Hackamore Jim — if he ever had any other name I never knew it — where he hailed from nobody ever knew, but he could ride any horse that wore four feet. I have been told that a few times in his life he came out second best, but no one ever said that Hackamore Jim couldn't ride.

Hackamore Jim arrived in town one day riding a little buckskin broncho that was about the best rope and cut-out horse that had ever been worked in the stockyard pens. Jim kept his horse out on the Clark Ranch a couple of miles down the river. He had been in town a few days when he went to Pete Nelson and arranged for a horse race. Horse racing with Jim was a prime sport.

It was agreed that the race would start two miles out of town on the Old Fort Keogh road and finish in front of the Milligan Hotel on Main Street. Any cow pony was eligible. There must have been at least twenty-five cow ponies lined up on the starting line, and crowds of cowboys, ranchers, soldiers, and Indians lined both sides of the road from the starting place to the finish. Bets of all kinds were placed on the various ponies, and no less than a hatful of silver dollars was the purse for the winner.

Hackamore Jim had chosen a young Crow Indian boy to ride his horse. The young Indian was riding bareback, and made a picture long to be remembered, as he sat on the buckskin, a couple of eagle feathers tied in his long black braids, and wearing a breech clout and a pair of beaded moccasins. His face was stern with excitement.

The buckskin stood near the outside of the line with his head down; ears lopped foreward and sleepy-eyed, he looked about as interested in that race as a contented cow under a shade tree. I almost expected to see him fall asleep before they got the rest of the horses lined up for the start. Then the pistol roared and they were off. That piece of buckskin came to life and unwound like a ball of yarn. He started down the road like a scared jack rabbit. The young Indian lay down along the pony's back, scarcely visible, and never made a move until the buckskin sailed past the hotel a half dozen lengths ahead of the nearest second. There was no chance for argument in that race, the buckskin safely and easily took the honors and the hatful of silver dollars.

Hackamore Jim took his horse back to the Clark Ranch and returned to town to celebrate. He and his friends made the rounds of every place in the town boasting a French mirror and a brass footrail, but a couple of days later he emerged from a faro game with his pockets turned wrong side out. He walked the two miles to the ranch to see his horse, and then returned to town.

He again went to Pete Nelson, this time to arrange a raffle for his horse. One hundred chances were sold at one dollar each in about two hours' time. Doc Willis won the horse and offered it to Nels Hansen without even seeing it. Nels offered Doc $75 for the horse, and Doc closed the deal. Next day, Nels went out to the Clark Ranch to see the horse. He came back to town, and arranged another raffle, this time selling sixty chances. Leo Holmes, a photographer, won this time, and he went to see his horse and returned to town rather annoyed. He raffled the horse again, and Otto Mosby, the town's leading tailor, won it. I knew Otto well and knew he had no place to keep a saddle horse, and no use for one, so I hunted him up and offered him $40 for the buckskin. Otto never bothered to look at his property, but gave me a bill of sale and took the $40. Several people asked me to put him up for raffle again, but I wanted the horse, so I declined. Had I put it up, the horse raffle might have gone on indefinitely. I told Pete Nelson I had bought the horse, and intended to keep it. I still have it — beautifully tanned — on the floor in front of my fireplace.

When I arrived at the Clark Ranch to claim my horse, Chang Yoo, the Chinese cook, told me the buckskin had dropped dead from over-exertion in the long race shortly after Hackamore Jim had brought him back to the ranch!

Western Hospitality

THE CATTLE AND SHEEP RANCHERS OF THE WEST WERE KNOWN the world over for their generous hospitality. They were given to sharing the best they could offer to the wayfarer or the casual passerby. This was always cheerfully extended to all who passed their way, whether he be the wealthy cattle baron or the lonesome cowboy, who carried his sole earthly possessions on his pony's back. The rancher might claim the brand seen only on half a hundred steers or he could be lord of every hoof on a thousand hills, yet neither his appearance nor the grandeur of his ranch home seldom would betray the difference, and in the branding corral you wouldn't know the owner from any one of his cowboys.

The unwritten law of hospitality of the Western range country was also a law of necessity. With scattered ranches located where feed and water were abundant, it often was a day's journey to visit the domicile of a neighbor. The mounted traveler often carried his bedroll but seldom his bacon and coffee. He slept in his own blankets wherever night overtook him, but he knew that no rancher, miner, trapper, or cowboy would refuse to extend the hospitality of a meal, and should the owner of the camp or ranch be absent for a time, the door might be closed but the latchstring always hung on the outside, and he was expected to make himself comfortable for as long as he chose to stay.

65

Many are the times I have been away from my ranch for days and weeks at a time and, upon my return, found that I had entertained numerous strangers and friends. Months afterwards, while at some distant ranch or town, some cowboy or rancher would mention his stay at the ranch at some time during my absence. Such instances were commonplace and I have yet to know of the code of hospitality ever being abused by any real Westerner.

One fall I had gone to Lewistown to purchase a six-horse load of provisions for the coming winter and had been on the trip a week. Returning home one evening about dusk, I turned in at the gate and noticed a light in the window and smoke issuing from the chimney. I thought nothing of this, and proceeded to unharness my horses, leaving the load standing near the ranch house. I fed my string team and refilled the manger of the traveler's horse. I did not recognize the saddle that hung on the harness peg, neither did I know the brand on the horse, so I took my guest to be from some distance. As I neared the house, I met the newcomer carrying in wood from the woodpile, his sleeves rolled up and his overalls covered with flour — telltale signs of some baking powder biscuits for supper.

When he saw me approach he opened the screen door. "Hello, stranger," he said. "Come on in and make yourself at home. Had your chuck?"

"No," I announced, "and I'm as hungry as a coyote." "Just in time," added my guest. "I have the stove covered with chuck — cookin' spuds, bacon, some fresh venison, a half dozen scrambled eggs, and the oven full of sinkers, and I just located a few dozen cans of eats under the bed, so we'll dine like kings tonight, partner. Been travelin' far?"

"Thirty miles since sunup," says I.

"Live near here?" he ventured.

"Yes," says I.

"It's getting late, better bunk up here tonight," invites my friend.

"I guess I will," I answered, and our friendship was made.

My stranger friend soon had the table covered with a heaping supply of good things to eat.

"Here's your artillery and feed bag, pard, sit down, put your feet under and wade in," he called, as he procured a plate and equipment from my cupboard in the corner back of the stove. We ate and talked for fully an hour, my guest and host was really a very creditable cook and to mention his artistic culinary skill with the biscuit dust is not to be omitted.

During our conversation I learned that my guest was from the Dakotas and was on his first visit to an uncle who had a ranch in the Judith Basin. After doing justice to everything on the table, we washed up the dishes and soon found ourselves chatting and joking as though we had been acquainted for years. My guest found a harmonica about the house and proved to be quite an artist. He was very interested in an array of Indian relics and curios covering the walls, and ventured many suppositions as to the owner of the display and ranch house in general — he even ventured to say that the owner evidently was a bachelor, as there was no evidence of a feminine touch either in the kitchen or the general appearance of the house. Although he did state that, for a bachelor, appearances were quite orderly.

He had not asked me my final destination and so far I had not volunteered the information. He kept up a continual conversation until the fire had long since died out and conversation turned to retiring for the night, and casually stated that, on the second day following, he would reach his uncle's ranch on Spring Creek, a few miles above Lewistown. Knowing many stockmen in that vicinity, I ventured to ask the relative's name, and was not a little surprised to learn that he was a casual acquaintance of mine. Furthermore, while attending the Stockmen's Convention a few months earlier in the season, a group of fifty or so had had their picture taken in front of the old Day House, a familiar hostelry of cattle and mining days, and I recalled that both his uncle and I had been in the group. Not thinking of myself as now being the unknown guest of my guest, I announced that I had his uncle's picture in my trunk at this very minute, and, reaching in my pocket for a key, proceeded to unlock a trunk near where we were sitting. As I produced the picture in question, he gave one glance at it and, leaping to his feet, exclaimed, "My heavens, pard, are you the hombre what lives here?"

Our friendship began that night, many years ago and lasted continuously until World War I, which saw us both in uniform. We trained together in Camp Lewis and a few months later I saw him for the last time as he sailed from Camp Mills, Mineola, Long Island, early on the morning of December 14th, 1917. During the war, we kept track of each other and wrote as often as occasion permitted, until a letter came from him stating that they were to go over the top next morning. My answer to this letter was returned to me months later, unopened, with the unfamiliar handwriting across its face "Killed in Action." The American Legion of Winnett, Montana, paid their last respects to a loyal comrade and a real hero by placing on their memorial hall the name of Carl Sandman, Post No. 95.

Another incident which I will never forget was during the days when cattle rustling was second only to cattle raising in eastern Montana. Our ranch was located at a junction through which the running and relaying of stolen cattle and horses between points in Canada and states farther south generally were routed.

Cattle rustlers were not an ordinary breed of men; their daring, courage, and strategy should have been put to a more honest and peaceful calling. To be caught stealing cattle on the Western range was likely to wind up at the end of a lariat, and no rustler intended to be a guest at a necktie party if he could help it. The rustler always was well mounted, and carried a six-shooter and often a Winchester, and could use both with unerring accuracy. Many of these men found it a profitable sideline to hold up an occasional bank or mail train, and the Overland stage, carrying the payroll to some mining camp, was also favorably considered.

One evening in late September, I was reading by the fireplace when I heard a rider approaching the house. As he dismounted and came up to the open door I could readily see that horse and rider were weary and dust covered from trailing long hours behind a herd. He wished to throw a small bunch of horses in a nearby pasture, and while he was driving his herd into the pasture I prepared supper for my guest. By the time the meal was on the table he was washed and waiting no second invitation. I could see he had had a long hard day in the saddle. After he had finished eating he helped with the few dishes and pans and our conversation drifted into the events of the day.

By the traditional code of the West one never asked a person's name, where he came from, or where he was bound; if he volunteered the information well and good, if not, no questions were asked. I have known many men, ridden with them, and lived with them for months, without learning their names or where they were from, and they asked as little concerning me. My guest chatted about every subject but himself, he was polite, well educated, and well mannered. There was only one slight flaw in his observance of Western etiquette — instead of removing his belt and gun upon entering the house he wore it the entire evening — and I noticed also that he never sat with his back to the door or window. As the hour grew late and we prepared to retire, I took the tarpaulin off and arranged the bed, and my guest removed his belt and gun and placed them conveniently on a chair at the edge of the bed.

I had contemplated sleeping on the front of the bed and my guest next to the wall, but the arrangement did not seem to suit my visitor. "Take the side next to the wall, tonight, if you don't mind," he said politely. I looked up questioningly just as he took a second .45 Colt from a holster under his calfskin vest and placed it under his pillow. I saw no reason to deny his request.

We had been sleeping for perhaps two or three hours when my guest, suddenly and quietly, sat bolt upright in bed with his six-shooter aimed directly at the door. His sudden movement awoke and startled me for the moment, but I did not move. I knew something was radically wrong, but what I did not know. My first thought was that if any fireworks began between my bed partner and someone outside, it would place me in rather a precarious situation. I wondered whether to stay frozen or melt and run down between the bed and the log wall.

Presently, I heard steps on the ground in front of my open door. My guest kept his gun pointed in the direction of the noise, but remained motionless. In the stillness, I faintly heard the munching of grass near my porch and my heart beat again as I realized that my saddle horse was in the yard in front of the door and was peacefully eating grass. I said nothing, and my friend must have recognized the cause of the sound at the same time I did, as he quietly replaced his gun under his pillow and soon we were both sleeping peacefully again.

After an early breakfast, my unknown guest was again on his way. He was driving a herd of some forty to forty-five very fine horses, representing at least a dozen different brands. He mentioned nothing of the disturbed quiet of the night and I doubt if he ever knew that I had been awakened.

After I saw him disappear over the hill, still trailing in the dust of his horses, I returned to the ranch house to complete my morning's work, and while making up the bed I found under his pillow a black silk bandana, in the corner of which was neatly tied a twenty-dollar gold piece. My guest had wished to pay for his night's lodging and devised this way of doing so. Just two days after this episode I received another visitor in the person of a United States Marshal and two deputies who were on the trail of a notorious highwayman wanted for a stage holdup and the recent shooting of two men in a cattle-rustling fight.

I recognized from their description that it was none other than the amiable lone rider who had been my guest a few evenings before. I had heard and read numerous accounts of his daring exploits of banditry, but this was my first opportunity to meet this acknowledged king of cattle rustlers. Although I do not recall seeing any notches on the handle of his gun, I had long known that several could rightfully be cut there. He had done me no harm, and my long-kept motto of "See no evil, hear no evil, and speak no evil," bade me say adieu to my trio of silver stars as I saw them trotting off in the opposite direction from that taken by my lone guest of a few days before.

About a month following this incident, I picked up a Montana newspaper and saw where this same lone bandit had held up a bank in a small mining town. A posse was soon made up and followed in pursuit. They surprised the lone rider about sunrise in a blind canyon, and a running gunfight ensued, in which the bandit and two of the posse were badly wounded. The bandit was tried and sentenced to a life term in the state prison at Deer Lodge but due to failing health, after serving fifteen years, he was pardoned, in 1924.

The same year, during a trip to Cuba, I was not a little surprised to meet this same knight of the range on the streets of Santa Clara and was pleased to accept an invitation to the plantation estate of an older brother. Again, some two years later, I was sitting in my car one afternoon in East San Diego, California, when the same man came smiling up to me, and introduced me to his bride of a year, inviting me to dine with them at their beautiful little orange ranch near La Mesa. Since he is now a most respected citizen, happily married, and living at peace with the world around him, I will not venture any names, but still claim him as a most genial and admirable friend.

There are few pioneers of Montana who have not at some time seen the famous N Bar brand on some of the many thousands of horses and cattle that roamed over the hills of central Montana. This ranch, located near the quiet little city of Grass Range, was owned by the late Thomas Cruse, and comprised some fifty thousand acres of land. Something over thirty thousand sheep were sheared on this ranch and I have known of as many as forty cowboys, herders, and ranch hands to be quartered at the N Bar bunkhouses during the roundup and branding season.

The story of how the late Tommy Cruse drifted into Fort Benton seventy years ago, penniless and hungry, is well known to every pioneer of the state. The lure of gold had brought him to the West. A poor shoemaker shared his humble cabin and bread with the homeless and hungry boy and later grub-staked him to a miner's pan, burro, and enough food to last him a month in the mountains. The agreement was fifty-fifty, and a farewell handshake was the bond.

Thirty days later, Tom returned to report a strike, and file location notice for himself and cobbler partner. This partnership sold out twelve months later for one hundred thousand dollars cash, half of which the shoemaker received, for faith in a burro and the word of an honest prospecter. With this first venture, Tom Cruse started on a successful career that, within forty years, gave him mines and ranches totaling in value more than three million dollars.

One day in the fall of 1912, we were putting up hay at our ranch and my brother, Lone Eagle, suggested I go to town to pick up a couple of extra men to run the bull rakes. It was haying season on most of the large ranches and help was scarce. The one street in town seemed quite deserted as I walked leisurely up one side and down the other, looking for an idle man. The only persons I could see at the time who seemed not too busy were a white man and a half-breed Indian, talking at the edge of the sidewalk. The white man wore overalls tucked into a pair of dusty cowboy boots, a flannel shirt, and a battered Stetson hat. At any Eastern railroad yards he would probably have been told to move on.

I walked leisurely up to the stranger and asked him if he would be interested in a few weeks' work in our hayfield. He turned toward me with a friendly smile, stating that he was sorry but he would be busy the rest of the week. He added that he, also, was having difficulty in securing men for his own haying crews and asked me if I knew where he could hire twenty-five or thirty more hands for the next six weeks to assist him in putting up three thousand acres of alfalfa on his own ranch. I looked him over, but made no reply. I was puzzled to know whether he was kidding me or whether he had been among the woolies a few years too long. I walked on into the post office, and asked the postmaster the status of the man outside, and was informed that he was Tom Cruse, millionaire owner of the N Bar Ranch.

The story of how this same cattle baron returned a practical joke played on him by several close friends is well known. It was after the N Bar fall roundup that the usual trainload of fat beef steers was shipped to the stock yards at Chicago. It was always a gala event and lucky were the dozen or so cowboys who would be selected to accompany the shipment. After the cattle were unloaded and sold, the genial Mr. Cruse would pay the boys their fall wages with a liberal bonus and allow them a ten-day stay in the metropolis. In most cases, they would return to the ranch with many tall tales of their adventures and generally down to their last buck.

On the day of the N Bar's arrival, the beef market was tops and everyone was in a happy mood. While window shopping on one of the main thoroughfares, several of the boys spied Mr. Cruse leisurely walking down the street ahead of them, dressed in his usual not-too-well-kept ranch clothes. About the same time they also spied a uniformed policeman in the block, walking his beat. This could be a lot of fun for the boys and a good joke on the "old man," so they approached the cop and, most sincerely, told him that the old man had accosted them several times panhandling for dimes and a few drinks. The well-meaning policeman, believing their story, immediately picked up the old gentleman and took him to the police station. The cattle baron was pretty much put out at this unprovoked treatment and upon reaching the station told them off in no uncertain words, but to picture him as being a multimillionaire was a bit beyond the imagination of the police. However, Mr. Cruse managed to talk the police chief into calling several of the officers in the exchange bank where he was in the habit of depositing his cattle checks in amounts that would stagger most of the bankers themselves, and soon proved that he was not a panhandling bum. In no time, he had received the apologies of all the police staff, but the incident did not end here.

He soon found out why he was accused of begging dimes and it was just thirty minutes to train time when he was graciously escorted back to the railroad station. He made one or two calls to his Chicago banker, where the boys were to be paid off, instructing the teller to inform the boys that they would all be welcome back at the N Bar Ranch, if and when they arrived. It was a sorry looking bunch of waddies that met at the exchange bank the next morning; their little joke had really boomeranged that time and it was a long and tiresome ride back to Montana in that old cattle car. We didn't see much of Chicago that trip, but the baron was all smiles when he greeted us at the breakfast table the morning of our arrival at the old N Bar Ranch.

Chapter VIII

Early Cree Rustlers in Montana

SOON AFTER THE DISCOVERY OF GOLD IN MONTANA AND THE Black Hills country of western Dakota, the long caravans of covered wagons began to trek westward from the cities and farms of the East. This steady stream of the Paleface wagons was of much concern to the Indians, for the treaty made with them by the United States government, in 1868, had given the Sioux all the Black Hills as their hunting ground. But when gold was discovered, treaties were forgotten and the buffalo were being driven from the prairies and slaughtered by the thousands. The Indians were not long in seeing that their source of meat supply was soon to vanish from the plains. They sent delegation after delegation of chiefs to Washington to protect their treaty rights, but each summer brought more of the white settlers.

The Indians' appeal to the Great White Father had availed them nothing. Then they warned the long trains of white-covered wagons, but when the hordes kept moving steadily west, the council fires of the Sioux could be seen as great chiefs called their warriors together. The pipe of peace was passed from warrior to warrior, but they all shook their heads. "War!" "War!" was the answer.

At sunrise, hundreds of yelling painted warriors rode their ponies into the midst of sleeping white caravans — thus began the bloody Indian wars of the West. The Indian had taken his last stand to hold the land of his fathers and the home fires of his children. For years to come, no white man or no Indian knew whether the cloud of rising dust in the distance was friend or foe.

For protection of the ever-increasing number of travelers, the United States government found it necessary to establish forts along the most important trails of the frontier. These isolated places of refuge were garrisoned by a company or so of mounted soldiers, scouts, and hardy plainsmen. Most of the Indians were hostile to these outpost forts, yet, there were always a few so-called friendly Indians and half-breeds in every community. In many instances, these Indians were employed as scouts and couriers.

Perhaps no Indian fort in Montana was better known, in the early days, than old Fort Musselshell, which was built at the mouth of the Musselshell River. This famous fort and trading post was established in 1866, under the name of Kerchival City. It was used mainly as a protection for wood choppers who furnished the fuel for the "Far West" and other river steamboats, which brought supplies and passengers from St. Louis to Fort Benton and Great Falls. Kerchival City washed away in the spring of 1868 and was rebuilt the following summer, under the name of Fort Musselshell. A company of soldiers was sent from Camp Cooke that same year and established a barracks under the name of Camp Reeve. On May 9, 1869, the fort was attacked by Indians, and thirty-six soldiers and Indians were killed in the ensuing battle. This fort was maintained until 1874, when it was finally abandoned.

Soon after Fort Musselshell was built, it became necessary to purchase a number of horses. Several half-breed Cree Indians, who were camped within sight of the Fort, offered to sell the commanding officer the required number of horses. The average Indian pony owned by the Crees would not meet the requirements of the Army horse. However, this small band of Crees were riding some exceptionally fine animals, so a bargain was struck to purchase the horses meeting the specifications, which partly filled the requirements of the post. The Crees, desiring more of the Paleface golden eagles, offered to bring more horses if the commanding officer would just give them a few days' time. This was agreed, and the next day found the Cree braves disappearing across the prairies toward the south. The sun had not risen and set more than could be counted on two hands, when a moving speck was seen one evening, on the horizon, an hour or so before sunset. As the moving speck drew nearer, it proved to be the Crees returning, driving a small band of fine horses. The horses were duly inspected by the commanding officer, and, almost without exception, were passed on and paid for.

The soldiers were well pleased; the Crees were elated. Then, if the Crees could bring six more horses as good as the rest, more glittering golden eagles would gladly be exchanged. After a few days of resting and feasting, the red-skinned plainsmen headed their ponies over the rolling prairies a second time. Five suns passed, and still another five suns had risen and set, and yet no braves returned. Half a moon waned in the heavens before the sentinel announced the sight of horsemen in the distance riding directly toward the great stockade as fast as their ponies would carry them. They did not look like the party of friendly Crees, as now but three galloping riders could be counted, while seven had left the fort.

Presently a volley of shots was heard in the distance, followed by the appearance of half a hundred yelling warriors. Commands to be in readiness at the Fort were given. The fort was being attacked by the Indians. On and on the yelling warriors rode, shots were fired and feathered arrows dropped close behind the three lone riders, then one of them leaned far backward and, swerving from his horse, fell to the ground. Only two succeeded in reaching the great stockade gate, yelling and begging to be let in. Recognized by the soldiers as the friendly Cree scouts, the great wooden gates swung out, and closed, just as the yelling band of Crows made a wide swing and circled clear of the range of the rifles behind the massive wooden walls.

The Crow Indians were the most peaceable tribe in Montana, and owned the finest horses. Plenty Coups, their brave and respected chief, was always friendly to the whites and his word and friendship were never broken. The cause of the war party was now evident. The Crows had missed several of their finest horses and while getting on the trail left by the Cree rustlers, the Crows had caught up with the raiding party with their six stolen horses. A running fight had not only recovered the six horses, but had sent five Cree horse thieves to the Happy Hunting Grounds.

Chapter IX

The Scaffold Indian Burial

IT WAS THE CUSTOM AMONG THE NORTHWEST PLAINS INDIANS to bury their departed tribesmen in cemeteries or burial grounds located on prominent hills in the vicinity of their camps. The graves, with no identification whatsoever, usually were three to five feet deep and covered over with stones to keep wild animals from burrowing into them. Even with no identification, each grave was known by the deceased's relatives, and reverenced by all.

Those individuals who, by deeds of valor, had become heroes and chiefs, were entitled to the more elaborate scaffold burial. This scaffold consisted of four poles some ten or twelve feet in length, set upright in the ground, at the top of which was woven a platform or cradle for holding the body of the Indian. This platform was constructed of wooden poles and rawhide. In the timbered areas, the platforms often were built right in the limbs and branches of large trees. There also have been a few Indian burials on natural shelves or layers of rock along high cliffs or mountain sides.

Nearly always the deceased warrior's favorite dog or horse, or both, was slain and placed near the scaffold, and it was believed that their spirits, too, entered the Happy Hunting Grounds with their masters. Prepared food also was left near the warrior to be used until he should reach that Indian paradise where all game would be plentiful. The devoted wife of the departed warrior also has been known to have sacrificed her own life to go to the Happy Hunting Grounds with her husband. For some time after the weird rites and wailing cease, the body was closely guarded from wandering marauders. A sentinel was placed nearby in some concealed spot near the scaffold to watch it. Any traveler might view it from afar, or at the scaffold itself, but if any attempt was made to molest it, in any way, an unmistakable warning was given to the intruder.

Once, Lone Eagle and I were riding through the old Fort Berthold Indian Reservation in Montana, when we noticed, in the distance, a scaffold burial. We rode over to the scaffold and, still seated in our saddles, surveyed the gruesome bundle of buffalo hides covering the remains, perhaps of a warrior. Riding around it several times, we concluded it must have been there many years, and being curious as to its history, we dismounted and climbed up to more closely examine its contents. I was perched high on Lone Eagle's shoulder, when we heard a rifle shot in the distance. We paused; a few moments passed and then, thinking it must be some passing hunters, we resumed our investigation by trying to tear off some of the buffalo hides. Another shot was fired, this time the bullet singing close to our ears. A third warning was not necessary. It took us no time at all to get to the ground, mount our ponies, and leave our departed Indian brother to repose in peace and quiet on his wind-swept bier.

Black Butte near Lewistown, Montana, is a famous landmark which can plainly be seen over an area of a hundred square miles in eastern Fergus County. This mountain, some five or six miles across, and rising perhaps five thousand feet above the surrounding benchland, is always black, even in winter, when the snows have covered every other part of the state. I have seen the snow many feet deep, and temperature forty degrees below zero over the entire state while old Black Butte rose a mile above the surrounding country without a sign of snow on its majestic crest.

Perhaps the strangest Indian Burial places I ever chanced upon were the rimrock tombs on the south slope of Black Butte. These were a series of natural horizontal rock ledges or shelves formed by the erosion of the softer sandstone layers between. There were several shelves of this stone, about twelve or fourteen inches thick, with from twenty-four to thirty inches of space between them. In several places, the openings extended back six to eight feet and were from forty to fifty feet in length. Many years ago, some wandering tribe had buried several of their dead on the stone shelves. The bodies had been wrapped in buffalo skins and, due to the dryness of the air, they were in a very good state of preservation. How they were placed on the shelves was always a puzzle to me, as the shelves were cut in the sheer sandstone wall at least a hundred feet above any place a person could stand and it was at least forty feet from the uppermost shelf to the sloping bench above.

My attention was first called to this strange burial place when I was riding along on the trail below and noticed a dozen or so travoix poles and an old, weather-beaten Indian pack saddle lying on a huge boulder a few yards off the trail. Upon further examination of the vicinity, I found the remnants of what once was a wooden sled put together with rawhide thongs — a sled such as was used by the Plains Indians on winter marches. On describing this conveyance to David Hilger, State historian of Montana, years afterward, while visiting him in Helena, he informed me that it was the type of winter sled used by Chief Joseph and his band of Nez Perce warriors on their march through Montana in that memorable winter of 1877.

These implements of Indian journeying and the strategy of the surrounding country led me to believe that something of more than passing interest might be discovered in this strange array of tombs on the natural rock shelves. To scale the perpendicular wall was impossible, but I found that by covering a distance of perhaps four or five miles, I could circle the hill, and come back to them from above. This brought me to a point directly over, and about forty feet above, the shelves. I let my lariat down over the edge of the rimrock but, being alone, I had no safe way of securing the upper end of the rope, which was not more than forty-five feet in length. Deciding to explore farther, I slowly descended to the mesa below, pondering over what I had seen.

I returned a few days later, accompanied by Lone Eagle, and together we ascended to the rimrock directly above the shelves. We carefully surveyed our ground, and decided we could secure our ropes to the bench where we were and descend the forty feet to the rock shelf below. We used two ropes for safety. One was securely tied to a guide above, while a second rope, with body loops at both ends, was let down over the edge. I sat in one loop, and slid down the tied rope while my brother sat with feet braced against a rock, and slowly let me down, foot by foot.

The long narrow shelf proved to be interesting enough. Against the back wall were four large bundles, apparently just wrapped skins or buffalo-skin cases containing Indian burials. The other ledges were much narrower, and contained nothing. As we did not deem it safe for both of us to leave the top of the rimrock at the same time, we took turns exploring the small, low room containing the Indian mummies. As the space on the ledge was small, we decided to take one of the buffalo-skin cases out where we could examine it more thoroughly. I selected the oldest-appearing one, and tied it to one of the ropes, but we were unable to get it up to the top, as we could not maneuver it out around the edge of the ledge of the upper shelf, therefore it was necessary to lower it to the trail, about one hundred feet below. We had the two forty-five foot lariats which Lone Eagle unfastened from their ground moorings above and dropped down to me.

I placed a slip noose around the mummy, tied the two ropes together, and, securely bracing myself, I carefully worked the bundle over the edge of the shelf, and lowered it. Looking over the edge of the rock when I reached the end of the rope, I found the bundle still ten or twelve feet from the bottom.

It suddenly dawned on me that I was trapped on the rock ledge with my three mummy companions. I had no way to untie my mummy below, and to let go of the rope was worse still, so I was forced to sit on my narrow shelf and pull that 150 pounds of bones and buffalo skins back up.

I succeeded in getting it up to the shelf but could not pull it over the ledge. All the time my brother was no more than forty feet away, but helpless to assist me.

I was nearly exhausted, and was wondering what to do next, when Lone Eagle suggested that I cut the rope. (He would suggest that — it was my rope!) This procedure seemed pretty tough on my helpless warrior, but it was the only way out for me, and the quickest way down for the Indian. I cut the rope; then, coiling one length of rope for a weight, I threw the coil up to my brother. We were fortunate in this procedure, as he succeeded in catching it on the third trial, and, after resting a few minutes, I climbed to the bench above.

It took us some two hours to ride the five or more miles to where I had dropped the mummy. We carefully opened the outer case, and found it to contain three separate hides. The one on the outside was wrapped hair-side in, and the surface was still covered with dried pine pitch. It was difficult to take off even with the aid of our hunting knives. The next covering was greased, raw bull hide, while the inner skin was Indian tanned, and of a light yellow color, which probably was white when first tanned. It contained the remains of the Indian. The flesh had completely dried away, only a few patches of dried skin remaining on the skull. The clothing, made of deerskin, was in a fair state of preservation, but no personal possessions were found.

The inner buffalo skin, the deerskin clothes, and the skull we carried away with us, leaving the rest there. I have often wondered if, after forty years, the other three warriors are still resting in their niche on that ledge up on the south slope of Black Butte.

I recall a humorous incident connected with the relic we brought back from Black Butte. We were entertaining a guest at our ranch — a returned missionary from China. This native Chinese lady had been a college classmate of my parents back in New Jersey. She had returned to her native land, became the head of a Chinese girl's college, and, after many years of service, was making a tour of Europe and America in behalf of her beloved school. I also had recently been graduated from college, and had not as yet decided definitely on my future career. Being by far the brightest and most saintly child in my uncle's immediate family (they had no children of their own), our good missionary guest emphatically decided, for me, that I would be a good representative and most shining example of my illustrious family if I were to become a missionary among the Chinese — I had this urgent request thrust upon me at breakfast, at dinner, and at supper, for two hours every evening before I could go to bed, and between meals. For two weeks I heard so much about the needs of the Chinese that I could think of little else. When I returned from our Indian expedition, I proudly exhibited part of our treasure, but the Indian skull I cached in a box in the woodshed. One day, I showed part of the collection to our guest, but it was anything but interesting to her. She even insisted that I take the "horrid things" back and put them exactly where I found them, and that I "should leave the dead alone," but I had had too much trouble getting them, so I put them out of sight.

The continual chant of the well-meaning Chinese guest had begun to wear on my nerves, and one evening after an especially long-drawn-out talk, I retreated to the woodshed for solitude and quiet. While contemplating the lecture my eyes fell on the gruesome countenance of my Indian skull. It startled me just enough to give me an idea, and I thought I could detect a faint smile on that deep-eye-socketed, bony face, that spurred me on to plan out my scheme.

Our distinguished guest had been given my room while visiting us, and I had taken another, but I knew even to the one squeaky board in the floor, the exact spot of the old wooden beadstead with its low foot, and high head, and, then, there were no locks on any door. I stood quietly outside my

mand — their great and honored chief must be taken, at once, back to the land of his forefathers from whence his soul had departed to the Happy Hunting Grounds. My friend and his staff of museum officials tried to reason with them — tried to persuade them to leave their chief where the paleface brothers could also do him honor. They even offered the Blackfeet large sums of money to let the warrior remain in his place of royal state, but all their pleadings and offers fell on deaf ears; the braves could not be bribed by the white man's gold. The chief must be taken back at once to the homeland and even to the same sturdy cottonwood by the riverside.

And so, I was obliged to escort the Blackfeet warrior back to the land of his fathers, back to the great cottonwood sentinel on the bank of the old Missouri. Even today, I can safely vouch for the fact that the old chief of the Blackfeet still rests in peace in the land of the Missouri and the Musselshell.

Chapter X

The Cowboy

THE WESTERN COWBOY, IN HIS NATIVE GARB, IS, PERHAPS, THE most picturesque figure in all America. He belongs to a class of men unequaled in courage, skill, daring, and horsemanship. Like the American Indian and frontiersman, he is entirely self-sufficient in any situation. Alone on the plains or in the mountains, he survives where others perish.

Every part of the cowboy's clothing and equipment is necessary and useful in his everyday work. The highly-prized broadbrimmed hat is the pride of his personal wardrobe, and the standard of distinction for the cow country of the West. A ten-gallon Stetson is the cowboy's passport in any Western society. These great hats, of finest beaver felt, are the best known protection when the hot summer sun beats down, and it is not unusual for one of these hats to be worn continuously in all weather for ten to twenty years. Where can forty-five to sixty dollars be spent more economically? Many are the times I have dipped a cool drink from some desert spring, in the outer rim of my hat, and then filled the inside to carry a drink to my thirsty saddle horse.

The turkey red or black silk neckerchief also was an added protection from the sun, but its real use was to cover the face when trailing the herd over long miles of dusty alkali plains. By completely covering his face with his closely woven silk bandana, practically all the fine, burning alkali dust was excluded from the eyes and nose of the cowboy, while breathing was unobstructed and visibility was always good. The bandit also noted that a person thus wearing his neckerchief over his face was difficult to identify, and made use of this means of disguise in his daring exploits. However, he usually brought the neckerchief mask down below his eyes, for better vision in case he was suddenly forced to resort to his own weapons in his unlawful exploits.

The cowboy's shirt usually was of flannel, with, perchance, the addition of a leather vest in cooler weather. His Levis were likely to be supported by a belt of his own workmanship in braided leather or colored horsehair, often adorned with an assortment of silver spots and conchas.

Next to his ten-gallon hat, his boots are perhaps the most costly and prized items of the cowboy's wearing apparel. Justin and Hyers were among the standards in cowboy footwear, and no cowboy's equipment could be complete without a pair of these sturdy, high-heel riding boots. They were, and are, the most practical footwear a cowboy can have. Every distinctive design of the boot has its specific purpose for the safety and comfort of the rider. The narrow toe is a safety measure. Where a walking shoe might catch in the stirrup and drag the unfortunate wearer behind a wild mount the narrow-toed boot will slip easily from the stirrup. The high tops were a protection against weather, brush, and rattlesnakes, and presented a smooth surface to the saddle fenders. The high, sloping, undershot heels had the dual purpose of giving one a secure position in the hickory ox-bow stirrup without the danger of letting the foot slip through. They serve also as an anchor in soft corral or prairie dirt when the cowboy has to brace or hold anything on the other end of a lariat.

The heavy spurs, with their spoked rowels, are more than helpful when the cowboy's hands are full and quick action from his cut-out horse is needed. A whip or quirt is worse than useless in the corral. The horse is trained to have a lariat loop swung over his head without displaying the least fear from the whirring rope, and would detect no difference between a rope and a whip, were he accustomed to an occasional cut from a quirt.

Most of the cowboys carried the old reliable Colt six-shooter, of heavy calibre, when I first rode over the ranges of Montana and the Dakotas in the early 1900's. It was carried in an open holster on a belt, hung low so that the handle was handy when the hand was lowered naturally. The holster usually was tied down by a rawhide string around the leg to keep it from coming up with the gun on a quick draw. And don't misjudge the cowboy who may be seen carrying his Colt .44 every time he is riding the range. He is not the trigger-happy bad man you read about. He is not looking for trouble or expecting to meet a war party over the next hill. He is carrying the proverbial "shootin' iron" for his own safety and the protection of his riding companions and livestock.

Twice in my own experience I have been forced to shoot horses to save the lives of my friends or myself. My first experience of this kind was during a spring roundup in the Flatwillow River country. Another cowboy, called Shorty, and myself were riding the morning circle, and he was breaking a new horse, which was being ridden for the first time. The day was quite cold and Shorty had worn a pair of heavy rubber overshoes over his boots to keep his feet warm. Without warning, his horse made a lunge, and proceeded to go into a long series of fancy gyrations that eventually unseated his rider. One foot hung in the stirrup and Shorty was being dragged by his wildly pitching horse. Then the horse gave several vicious kicks, one of which caught him squarely between the shoulders, his heavy, sheepskin-lined mackinaw being all that saved him from a broken back. A few seconds' time, just then, could have meant life or death to the unfortunate rider. As he was being dragged on the side of the kicking horse nearest me, my only chance was to take a quick aim at the plunging horse's head and shoot him. Since both the horse and Shorty, now unconscious, were in a moving, jumbled mixup, it was risky, but I had to take the risk, and quickly. So I fired twice in rapid succession at the horse's head and he immediately took a nose dive and landed dead across the cowboy's legs. Shorty was badly bruised and still unconscious when I got to his side. I was obliged to use my horse and rope to ease the dead broncho off his legs. However, a couple of months around the bunk-house with a pair of homemade crutches and Shorty was back in the saddle again, as good as ever.

My second experience includes the unusual medical knowl-edge of an elderly Crow Indian grandmother. Lone Eagle and I were out one day in the late fall, looking for some stray horses. I was riding a green broncho which I had selected to break as a rope horse. After riding for some time, we sepa-rated in order to cover two coulees some distance apart, agree-ing to meet at a designated point on the river.

After perhaps an hour I came to a narrow creek, spanned by a short log corduroy bridge, which had been built as a wagon-crossing. My horse had never crossed a bridge before and when his foot hit the logs the strange sound frightened him and he suddenly whirled around. I wanted to get him used to crossing bridges, so, stroking him gently, I tried again to get him on the bridge, but at the first step on the logs he reared and bolted. After a little more waiting I tried again to induce my green broncho to cross the bridge. As he again reared up suddenly, the large bridle buckle on top of his head struck me squarely on the chin and knocked me backward. I must have tightened up on the bit, and his hind feet slipped on the wet ground and he came over backwards so suddenly that I could not swing out of the saddle in time, and we both landed in a heap on the ground.

I was somewhat dazed from the blow on my chin and when I realized what had happened I saw that my boot was still in the stirrup under the horse. My horse then made a lunge to get up and I knew that if he did, I would be unable to get up in the saddle, as my leg was numb and stinging. My first thought was that, should he get to his feet, he would start kicking and drag me, so I pulled on the one rein to hold his head down so he could not get to his feet. He was lying on my leg and hip, but I dared not try to move or let him move. I knew I could not hold on much longer, and my only chance was to shoot him where he was. My gun was still in the holster and luckily was on the upper side where I could reach it without difficulty. So, still holding tightly to my horse's head by the one rein, I placed my .38 as close to the horse's temple as possible, and fired. After a few struggles, he stretched out, still on top of my leg. My entire leg was cold and numb, and I was quite shaken up. It was fully an hour before I succeeded in uncinching my saddle and, by pushing and pulling, I finally freed myself from under my dead horse.

My leather chaps had protected my leg from scratches, but my foot had been caught in the wooden stirrup, which was twisted sideways and broken by the weight of my horse. It was swelling badly, when I stepped on my foot it was as numb as a piece of wood. It was at least two miles to the nearest ranch house on the river. Slowly I made for it along the creek road and had gone not more than a quarter of a mile, when I saw a lone rider on the ridge above me. I shot twice to attract his attention, and as soon as he saw me he came on a gallop to my assistance. He took me to the ranch house and then, borrowing another horse from the rancher, he went back after my saddle.

The ranch belonged to an old-country German and his Crow Indian wife. This elderly Crow grandmother cut my boot up the front and then cut up a deerskin in one long strip some four inches wide by cutting around and around the hide until she had one long band of buckskin. This she put into a pail of water for a few minutes and then, wringing it out with her hands, she wrapped it tightly around my foot and ankle until it was as large as a football. Then she arranged me in a chair so that my foot was on the oven door of the kitchen range. For two hours the oven heat shrunk this bandage of deer skin, then she removed it, soaked it again, and repeated the process all that evening and for several days following.

In the meantime, the cowboy who had brought my saddle

to me went down to the appointed spot to tell my brother of my mishap.

I was at this old German's ranch for nearly six weeks, while his faithful Indian wife attended to my broken foot. Some years later, in Lewistown, when I was enlisted in the first world war, the examining physician noted a couple of scars on my foot and asked the cause. I told him of the incident and how the old Indian grandmother had set my broken foot in the primitive Indian way. After several X-rays, he told me that no modern medical method could have accomplished any better results than did the elderly Crow woman.

Perhaps the cowboy's chaparajos, or "chaps," are among the most picturesque items of his everyday attire. These leather breeches or leggings were first used in the brushy Southwest Big Bend cattle country as a protection to the cowboys' legs and trousers. The plain leather chaps are generally of the fringe or batwing type. The wide batwings furnish a place for a little personal decorating — initials, ranch brand, or some special design in inlaid colored leather. Angora chaps are favored in the northern country, as a protection against the cold winter weather. The natural black and white skins are sometimes varied by dying the white angora hair a golden sunset or red shade. When the cowboy is mounted, the chaps, like the high-heel boots, are the ultimate in perfection and comfort, but to get caught afoot a half day's journey from your home corral, in either one, or both, would be the cause of a lot of uncomplimentary and sarcastic remarks.

The cowboy's saddle is a masterpiece in wood, steel, leather, and workmanship. It is personal property in every respect, and it generally is made to the owner's detailed specifications. Built to fit him like a pair of gloves, its strength and beauty of line are the pride and joy of any cowhand. Plain as a new shoe sole or beautifully hand stamped, it is perfect in design and workmanship. The plain leather job sets the cowboy back some forty to fifty dollars, but a full stamp job could cost several hundred. How these rawhide-covered saddle trees could stand up under a rolling half-ton horse, or take the sudden jerk from a running thousand-pound steer at the end of a forty-foot rope was always a marvel to me.

Up in our country could be seen any number of Meana and Ernst saddles, from Wyoming, and the Furstnow and Cogshell jobs were favorites from the Miles City shops. Saddles varied as to the swell of the fork and type of trees used. Rigging varied from three-quarters to center fire and double cinch, depending on the part of the country in which they were used. The boys from the level country liked the single-rigged saddle best, but in the hilly country the double rig was preferred. Some ropers liked a double rig, especially if they headed toward the rope, otherwise, they often had to ride the cantle in order to keep from tipping the saddle up in the back.

The bridle often was handmade of plaited leather or horsehair. The bridle bit usually was of long shank type, with bar across the lower end to keep the rope from getting caught between the two shanks and jerking the horse's mouth. The crossbar was of the spade design with brass roller.

The lariat, always an essential part of every cowboy's equipment, was made of three- or four-strand, hard twist, seven-sixteenths-inch fine manila or hemp rope and was from thirty to forty-five feet in length, the honda* generally was formed by splicing a small loop in one end and wrapping it with rawhide to take the wear.

Roping varied in different parts of the West, as well as with the individual roper. There were what we called "dally men" and "tie-fast ropers." The dally man would make his throw first, and when the loop was securely over the horns or feet, he would take a couple dallies† around the saddle horn and slow down until the rope tightened and the horse held on. This method took fast work on the part of the roper, to tie on before the animal took up the slack, but it had the advantage of not tying the cowboy to something he did not want.

* Small loop at the end, through which the other end of the lariat is passed to form a noose.
†Act of winding the rope around the saddle horn.

The tie-fast roper made his rope fast to the saddle horn before he made his throw. As soon as he had something in his loop he could stop his horse or jump off, as is done in rodeo calf roping, thus saving him the time of tying his dallies. This method had the disadvantage of occasionally tying the horse to some half-ton steer who had managed to get the rope around his shoulder or chest and could drag the horse instead of being stopped.

I became a confirmed dally roper quite early in my cowboy career, after a very bad throw at a yearling calf who happened to be running alongside his fourteen-hundred-pound grandsire. I missed the yearling just as grandpapa made a lunge right into my seven-foot loop, which tightened up over his shoulder and between his front legs — a padded ox yoke would not have given him any better pulling power. My rope was tied fast with no chance to untie it. When my horse saw that I had made a catch, he slid into a sudden stop and, before I realized my situation, that three-quarter-ton hunk of bull meat came to the end of my rope, and stood my nine-hundred pound cayuse and me right on our sky pieces. I was piled up between my own bronc and the whiteface bull. I finally made it back into my saddle again just in time for Mr. Bull to make another lunge at about a right angle to our former position. He succeeded in jerking my horse down on his side, where I also landed astraddle the rope, with the saddle at about half mast on my horse's side. The bull kept the rope taut, and I could not get my horse on his feet until the bull made for our general direction, when I managed to get the grounded saddle horse between me and the bellowing bull. My only course to relieve the situation was to saw my new lariat in two with my pocket knife. The last I saw of our bull, he was running across the flats with about thirty feet of my new black jack rope. Since then I have always been in favor of the dally method.

Occasionally, some of the boys carried a twisted horse-hair rope about twenty feet long, which they placed on the ground around their beds, hoping the bristly horsehair would keep any night-prowling rattlesnake from crossing over to their beds.

I recall an old-time roundup cook who always laid his black and white braided horsehair rope very carefully around his tarpaulin before he rolled in for the night. One morning, however, when rolling up his bedroll, he discovered a large diamondback rattler coiled up under the edge of his tarp. He very carefully examined the rope which still formed a complete loop on the ground around his bed and his long belief that a rattlesnake would never cross over a horsehair rope was shattered. However, he decided to give his ancient theory another test, so he carefully removed his bed without disturbing the coiled snake. We all stood back some distance from the snake and watched him with interest, when, a few minutes later, he slowly uncoiled and crawled over the braided rope as unconcerned as if he had been traveling down a smooth sand road. From that day on our veteran chuck wagon cook never bothered to encircle his roundup bed with the gaily colored horsehair rope.

The cowboy is so perfectly at home in the saddle that he can even sleep on his horse. Many are the times I have seen a cowboy companion, after a hard day's ride, coming in to the ranch soundly sleeping in his saddle, with only the occasional forward nodding and drooping of his head to indicate the rider was asleep. But let the horse shy, stop, or even change from his regular gait for a second, and the sleeping rider would instantly awaken with a quick tightening of his knees and alertness of his body.

I once made a trip from a neighboring ranch after a long day's ride in the saddle. I had stopped at this ranch for supper and started for home, a distance of perhaps ten or twelve miles, immediately after the evening meal. I rode up out of the river flats and onto the bench land toward home on one of my favorite rope horses which I had left at my friend's ranch for a few days, while looking for some stock in the vicinity. A horse will return to his home ranch, even after years of absence, though the distance may be several days' journey.

My little broncho could follow a trail at night as good as any hound dog, so I was confident that three or four hours would find us at the familiar Eagle Bar Ranch corral gate. I was tired, but my wiry mount had been resting for several days and was in the best of spirits, so I knew we should soon be home. After an hour or so I became very sleepy and, looping my bridle reins over the saddle horn, I placed my hands on the pommel and soon found myself nodding in short cat naps. I guess I was dreaming a little too much of the old high gate and my own cozy bed, because the next thing I knew my faithful little broncho stopped short and I awoke with a sudden start. I gathered up my reins, as before me loomed a high pole gate and corral bars, but somehow, they did not look familiar. It was not the corral gate of the Eagle Bar Ranch. In fact, I did not know where I was. I looked at my watch; it was 1:30 A. M. Four hours earlier I was well on my way along the Basin road, riding toward home.

After a few minutes' look around, I realized I was standing in front of the corral at the H Cross Ranch, where my faithful little mare was born and raised and where I had purchased her some eight months before. I was ten miles from the ranch I started from, and still twenty miles from home. Somewhere along the trail my horse had turned around and decided to return to her old home stamping ground, and I had been sleeping soundly in my saddle for over four hours.

The poncho slicker and perhaps a heavy wool blanket tied on back of the cantle, completed the cowboy's everyday equipment. He never carried less, and he needed no more. He often carried a Winchester carbine in a scabbard under the fender of his saddle, and many a coyote was eliminated from the landscape at the hands of these range riders.

Many incidents in the daily life of a cowboy are amusing to the casual looker-on, even though they may be fraught with danger. Lone Eagle and I were out in the north country badlands one day looking for some strayed cattle. We had divided on a ridge, to meet again in a coulee a couple miles down the creek, and Lone Eagle had located a small bunch of young dogies in a coulee near the place we had agreed to meet. In looking over the herd, he found one yearling that appeared to have a few feet of barbed wire tangled around one front leg, and wishing to remove the offending tangle of wire, he took down his rope and threw a loop over her head. He took a couples of dallies around the saddle horn, dismounted from his horse, and followed the forty-foot rope down to the animal at the other end. He decided he would have to throw the calf in order to remove the wire, but the calf proved to be a little too much for him to toss around easily. His broncho was holding the rope, as all good rope horses should, but the calf still refused to be downed in the somewhat vigorous wrestling match. Finally the calf decided to make a few fast circles around the horse, which Lone Eagle tried to halt by holding on to the rope some fifteen or twenty feet from the calf. However, the calf had made a couple of extra circles that were not taken into account by my brother — the circles being made only around Lone Eagle, while the calf dodged under the rope just ahead of the horse's nose. Then the calf returned to its former position and began a real tug of war with the ever-watchful broncho. My brother finally discovered that one of the rope loops was around his leg. And trying to extricate himself from the loop, he had fallen down and was pretty well tied up, about halfway between the prancing calf and his own horse. Every time he coaxed his horse up a few feet, the calf took up the slack and also took Lone Eagle along with her. Just about this time, I rode up over the brow of the hill and, seeing the tussle being staged below me, I hurried up to the scene to see what the play was. When I saw Lone Eagle sprawled out on the ground between the prancing calf and the stiff-legged cowpony, I burst out laughing. Then Lone Eagle began laughing as loudly as I. It was fully ten minutes before we could stop our hilarity long enough for me to put another rope on the calf and take the slack out of Lone Eagle's rope.

Chapter XI

Lone Wolf—The Sioux Scout

AS RELATED BY LONE EAGLE

THE AMERICAN INDIAN HAS THE UNDISPUTED REPUTATION OF being the best scout the world has ever known. On the Western plains in the early days the scout was, next to the war chief and medicine man, the most honored and respected man in the tribe and, in war time, the most important. Every tribe and band had their scouts, whose duty it was to watch for enemy approach and to find the location of enemy camps and war parties. During raids on neighboring tribes or settlements it was the scouts who made the perilous trip in advance to learn the strength of the party or to locate the ponies or other loot of war to be taken.

The scout either traveled alone or in pairs; rarely ever more than two were sent out together. His work was perilous and his life was always in danger. It was his craftiness against all the enemy, which in many cases numbered hundreds or even thousands of Indians, that saved his life in many instances.

His exploits and adventures were always far from his own people and many a narrow escape was made or daring fight won against great odds which had no witness except himself, and he seldom if ever spoke of it. On the other hand, many a lone scout was sent out by his chief on a reconnoitering expedition in enemy country who never returned to tell what happened.

On the frontiers of our Western states there were numerous Army posts where small detachments of soldiers were stationed for the protection of the pioneer settlers and ranchers against a possible attack from roving, hostile Indian bands. The majority of these forts consisted of a group of low log buildings and barracks built around a small court or drill grounds. Surrounding this group of clustered buildings was a stockade of ten- to twelve-inch logs set perpendicularly in the ground, forming a solid wall some fifteen to twenty feet high completely around the post quarters. At each of the four corners were the sentinel posts set slightly out over the stockade fence, which gave the sentinel a full view of the entire wall.

Every old-time officer who has commanded Army posts on our Western frontier knows of the valued services rendered by friendly Indians who were employed for scout duty. Among the many such Indians was Lone Wolf, a young man of the Oglala band of Sioux, who began his career as a scout for the government shortly after the close of the Civil War. Besides being a plainsman, he spoke half a dozen different Indian languages, which made him a valuable man as an interpreter when encountering Indians of other tribes.

Lone Wolf served as scout with such men as Generals Custer, Miles, Reno, Pratt, and Hugh L. Scott during the campaigns in the West, and always remained loyal to the government until his death on the Pine Ridge Reservation, in 1915.

Having known Lone Wolf since I was a small lad, I gained his most intimate friendship and thus heard many a true and interesting narrative of his life as an army scout. But perhaps one of the most remarkable feats of scouting he accomplished was the trailing of Antone La Pierre, a renegade Canadian half-breed. It was in the late fall of 1908 that the cowboys at the Horseshoe Bar Ranch had finished their horse roundup and were getting ready for the coming winter. They had rounded up some six hundred horses belonging to the oufit, which were to be kept on the range near the home ranch until spring. Among this bunch of range horses and Indian ponies were some fifty head of grade stock showing a marked strain of Morgan type. As these horses were in great demand for cavalry purposes, it was decided to run them on the range in a bunch by themselves where they could be broken during the winter and sold to the government the following spring. We herded them closely for awhile, but, as they did not seem inclined to graze far from the ranch, we became less watchful of their movements and only rode out to see them as we desired new mounts to be broken.

One day, however, several of the cowboys rode out to the herd for more horses but, on reaching the accustomed range, not a single one of the remaining twenty horses could be found. A general roundup was sent out a few days later, but not a trace of the Morgans could be found. They had been stolen and driven out of the country, leaving no clue to the direction they had been driven or to the thief.

Lone Wolf, who had long since retired from active service as an Army scout, having no tepee of his own, was an interesting and welcomed visitor among the ranch homes of the Dakotas and Montana. It was his custom to spend the winters on the various ranches in the Indian country and, as the warm spring days drew near, he would bid adieu to his friends and return to the camps of his people.

It was during the fall roundup on the reservation that we met up with the veteran scout and invited him over to the Horseshoe Bar to spend the winter. When we returned from hunting our stolen horses, Lone Wolf announced that, on the following morning, he would go in quest of the missing animals. He was then nearing seventy years of age, but insisted that he would find the stolen herd or capture for us, single-handed, twenty of the best wild horses that roamed the Black Hills country.

True to his word, Lone Wolf saddled up one of our best horses and, taking another for a pack animal, started out the next day in quest of the stolen horses. We watched him as he rode out of sight in the distance. A week went by and we received no word from our Indian friend. The Moon of Long

Nights (December) had come and gone, followed by the Snow Moon, with its usual blustery weather, and it turned steadily colder. The snow had piled in great drifts in the coulees and ravines on the bleak open prairies. We became uneasy about our friend, as we well knew the perils of being out on the prairies in the raging blizzards. But, as there were Sioux camped along most of the large rivers and many ranchers' homes dotted the prairies, it was likely that Lone Wolf would find shelter if traveling became difficult. One evening we were very much overjoyed to see the ranch house door quietly open and the stalwart form of the veteran scout standing in the light of the open doorway. We heartily welcomed our lone friend and after a warm supper invited him to a seat near the roaring fireplace, where he filled his red stone pipe and leisurely began to smoke.

"The Great Snow Maker has covered all the prairies with a deep blanket," I ventured to Lone Wolf as an introduction to conversation.

"Ugh; much snow and much cold are everywhere; Great Snow Maker makes hard travel for ponies," he ventured in return.

"We are happy to see you return alive from the furies of the frozen prairies," I said, in hope of drawing out the story of his quest for the stolen ponies. We sat in silence and eagerly watched his bronze face as he puffed away at his pipe of kin-ni-kin-nik. After many minutes of smoking and gazing into the crackling fireplace he began slowly to relate the story of his trip to the far north country.

The first two days were spent in locating the right trail, as there were so many small herds coming and going over the range near the Horseshoe Bar corrals that all trace of an outgoing herd was covered up by the numerous horse tracks. He had finally succeeded in discovering the right trail, which led directly south for a distance of fifty miles, and crossing the White River, led west through the Badlands, until it reached the western side of the Black Hills. There the trail of the twenty stolen horses and the mounted rider circled several times, and after crossing and recrossing the Little Big Horn River the trail turned in a northerly direction.

Lone Wolf carefully followed the trail through the rough Big Horn country and on into the alkali flats toward the north. The lone horse rustler seemed to know the country and was making good time driving the herd. Owing to the delay in starting and the difficulty in trailing over broken country, the rustler succeeded in keeping several days ahead of the lone Indian rider.

Many days passed and Lone Wolf still followed the trail toward the north, while the weather grew quite cold and light flurries of snow made the trail more difficult to follow. He was slowly gaining on his quarry and often found where the renegade had built his campfire only a few nights before.

He was nearing the Canadian border, just south of the Gros Ventre country, and was not more than two days behind the herd, when a cold northwest wind came up, bringing with it a blinding snow squall, which got worse as the hours passed until it became a raging blizzard which lasted three days. To go farther was impossible, besides the renegade was now in his own country and, not knowing that he was being followed, would hold the stolen horses in the Gros Ventre country until spring. Lone Wolf, confident that the herd and their driver could easily be found the coming spring, decided to return to the ranch with the information he had gained.

After a long and perilous ride over rough, windswept country and many days of suffering in raging snowstorms the half-starved Indian made his way across the mountains and prairies to the log ranch buildings of the Horseshoe Bar.

While Lone Wolf sat smoking his pipe in the glow of our blazing fireplace, he gave us a very vivid and exact description of the lone rider who had stolen our horses. Although the old scout had not once seen the horse thief, he knew his complete description, his habits, his home, his tribe, his age, and even knew the color of the horse he rode, and the kind of rifle he carried on his saddle.

Early the following spring four of our riders started for the

Gros Ventre country to try if possible, to locate the renegade thief and our stolen herd. The renegade, Lone Wolf had said, was a half-breed Cree Indian, about forty years of age, very short, but medium stocky, was crippled in left leg, wore Indian moccasins with spurs, a beaded buckskin shirt, corduroy trousers, and felt cowboy hat. He carried a .45 caliber revolver and a .30-.30 caliber short barreled carbine in a holster on the right side of the saddle. The rider also fired a rifle from the left shoulder and was generally left-handed. He was an excellent horseman and rider, used a heavy stock saddle, and rode a spirited gray horse when he drove the stolen herd to Canada. The renegade was experienced in horse rustling, besides being well acquainted with all of the surrounding stock country. He had lived with various tribes of Indians as well as among white settlers and knew the customs of each. Thus the old scout had given to us in detail the description of the rustler and the part of the country where he most likely would be found.

Our riders arrived at one of the Mounted Police posts and gained the assistance of a squad of Canada's scarlet horsemen. After several days of inquiry and search on the reservation, the renegade was located living with a family of half-breed Crees. He was arrested by the Mounted Police and an investigation made as to his identity and character. He proved to be Antone La Pierre, a notorious outlaw who was wanted in several states and provinces for horse stealing and other crimes. He was of French and Indian extraction and about forty years old, short of stature, and stocky.

Strange though it may seem, the outlaw answered to every item of description given by our Indian friend, Lone Wolf, and without this description, the capture of La Pierre would have been a long and difficult task. After La Pierre's arrest he told where the horses were being herded by some of his friends, about fifty miles north of the reservation. The entire herd was found and driven back to the Horseshoe Bar Ranch.

The vivid description of the renegade and his characteristics given us by Lone Wolf was a feat of scout work which demanded our highest admiration and it was not until he had explained his trip in detail that we could fully understand how he gained the detailed information about the wily half-breed. After much questioning and persistence he finally related the story.

"Cree half-breed knows all the country well, made ride in many ways to throw scout off trail, many circles across river show Cree been hunted many times before. Paleface make big campfire and get far away; Indian make little fire and get up close. Paleface no savvy how to sleep warm; Indian scrape fire in new place and spread blankets on warm ground. White man use many pans and plates to eat from; Indian use none. Indian make fire in hole in ground; paleface waste much heat. When half-breed camped for night he cut evergreen branches to lay blankets on; marks on ground where he slept showed he was very short and stocky; footprints on the ground around fire were moccasins. Paleface walk with toes pointed little out; Indian walk with toes straight ahead, and touches ball of foot first; white man steps heel down first. Indian's feet very flat while paleface has arched foot; half-breed had medium. Difference in tracks of left and right foot showed left slightly crippled. A spur rowel mark showed behind each moccasin track. Young man take long steps; old man take short steps and less steady."

Thus Lone Wolf in his broken English gave us his story of the unseen rustler. He went on further to explain how he found several bunches of white horsehair on the bark of trees where the rustler had tied his saddle horse and where it had rubbed its neck on the tree. Several times his horse had rolled in the dust, which showed the imprint of a large saddle and short carbine rifle holster strapped on the right side. This showed the rider to be left-handed. Also, on several occasions, he found empty .30-.30 rifle shells and judging from the position in which he found them, as related to the moccasin prints of La Pierre when he fired, they showed his rifle was fired from the left shoulder. The finding of several empty .45 caliber shells showed he carried a revolver of that caliber. When kneeling down to build his campfire the imprints of his corduroy trousers could easily be seen by the experienced eye. A number of small glass beads picked up once or twice where La Pierre had folded up his blankets showed the wearer's shirt to be of buckskin, as Indians rarely ever sew beads on cloth. That he rode a spirited horse was evident by the array of hoof prints on several occasions where his mount had reared and bucked with his rider. This also showed that he was an experienced rider. After reaching a certain point near the Canadian border, the direction in which La Pierre shifted his course showed plainly that he was headed for the Gros Ventre country and, with the severe weather and the belief that he was not being trailed, it was evident that he would not attempt to travel farther than the reservation. It was on these facts that Lone Wolf based his information and description of the lone renegade who had successfully driven a herd of stolen horses from Dakota to Canada, a distance of some seven hundred miles.

And to this day, if you should happen to meet any of the cowboys who have ridden the ranges of the Horseshoe Bar, they are certain to tell you of the trailing of Antone La Pierre by Lone Wolf.

Chapter XII

Lovers' Leap Rock
AS RELATED BY LONE EAGLE

SOME YEARS BEFORE THE HOMESTEADERS' CABINS WERE BEGIN-
ning to dot the cattle ranges of Montana, I was out scouting
for some cattle along the upper brakes and Badlands bordering the Missouri River. The country here is truly bad lands,
as its name implies — rough and rugged, yet wonderfully picturesque, and treacherous. From a narrow ridge looking down
into grassy coulees and rocky canyons, hundreds of feet below,
one finally works one's way down into a rock-walled canyon
where one may ride for hours up a narrowing gorge with sheer
rock walls towering high above. Miles farther the rider may
still be trying to figure his way out and into the next canyon.

Here and there is a hidden valley, widening out into a flat
bench containing hundreds of acres of the choicest grazing
land. If water is plentiful, nestled along the stream, or among
the cottonwoods or pines, will be the low, rambling, log ranch
house of some cattleman, truly in a little kingdom of his own,
and lord of all he surveys. A country seemingly carved out
of solid rock, yet vastly real and wonderful in its natural
ruggedness.

For days I scouted its ridges and picked my way up and
down its canyons, each night finding me sleeping close to my
campfire somewhere in the vastness of this majestic panorama
of God's great outdoors. Leisurely riding for hours in and out

of these mammoth canyons, I was certain of only one thing, and that was the fact that, no matter how winding or how long, eventually they reached and emptied into the great Missouri River, to the north.

At a particular point on the river, where I was emerging from a canyon and entering the widening valley in view of the river, there stands, on the western side of the canyon, a high rock cliff clearly seen from miles around. With a sheer perpendicular wall of perhaps two hundred feet, and not more than a stone's throw from the river edge, this cliff was once the favorite camping site of many an Indian band. It is located about a day's journey westward from the site of old Fort Musselshell at the junction of the Musselshell and Missouri rivers. Here, as evening overtook me, I made my camp at the foot of a cliff known as Lovers' Leap Rock. I remembered this place as I recalled the tragic story of the rock as told to me by my friend, Little Bear, veteran warrior of the Oglala Sioux, while we were camped here several years before.

It was the moon of Falling-Leaves (October) that Chief Oglala Fire, with his small band of Sioux warriors and their women and children, had killed many "ta-tan-ka" (buffalo), along the banks of Muddy Waters. The buffalo grass had been plentiful and the great shaggy animals were round and fat. The braves had encountered no difficulty in locating large herds feeding not far from their watering places and the women and children had been busy skinning and cutting the choicest meat for the winter's supply. The meat was all "jerked" and properly cured and the great hides had been staked down on the ground where the more experienced women scraped them, ready for the process of tanning for robes and tepee covers.

The buffalo which had been killed on the North Flats and bench lands of the river, had been prepared and brought across the river in buffalo-skin bull-boats tied to the tails of their ponies, which were led across by young Indian boys. Sometimes a swimmer would ride one pony and lead another, pulling the bull-boats, while others would hold on to their ponies and herd several at a time. It was all great fun, but required no little skill in crossing a quarter mile of treacherous current. The Indian camp was the scene of much work and activity and all had a hand in the task of storing the winter's meat, for did not Little Martin, the old gray-haired hunter, tell the children that the fur on the ermine was long and heavy and the beaver were working overtime on their houses — which was a sure sign that the coming winter would be long with deep snow.

Oglala Fire was preparing to make his winter camp in the sheltered valley of the Badlands, where the ponies would have plenty of buffalo grass on the southern slopes of the brakes. Not far from them, Yellow Dog and his band of over a hundred tepees had made their camp on Lodge Pole Creek, where they claimed the hunting grounds along the Musselshell, from the Flatwillow, on the south, down to the junction of the Musselshell and Missouri, on the north. Oglala Fire and Yellow Dog had hunted over the same buffalo grounds ever since they joined forces and drove the Blackfeet toward the north several winters before. In fact, Oglala Fire had wished to join the two camps as one, but neither of the chiefs desired to give his leadership to the other. However, their loyalty to each other in time of need was firm, and their friendship was never broken.

Yellow Dog had seen many winters come and go and he could no longer see to lead his young warriors on the warpath — his only son had been but recently slain in the battle of the Dry Big Horn in the fight against Red Wolf, and his grandson was yet a young warrior of not more than twenty summers, although he, even then, had shown great skill and daring as a buffalo hunter.

Oglala Fire was a great warrior, loved and respected by all his tribe. His tepee consisted of a devoted wife, and a beautiful daughter by the name of Silver Moon, who had come to Oglala's tepee one cold winter evening during the Moon-of-the-Long-Nights, eighteen winters before. Silver Moon was beautiful, and skilled in all the craft of the Indian girls. Her father was justly proud of his daughter, who wore beautiful beads and richly embroidered robes of white deerskin. She was the daughter of a chief, and by birth should be the wife of a chief, but Oglala Fire was often sad because he had no son, who by inheritance would become a chief.

Oglala Fire was ever desirous that some day the band of Yellow Dog and his band should be united as one. Soon Yellow Dog's place as chief would be taken by his grandson, Swift Arrow, and as the bands were on friendly terms, Oglala Fire wanted his beautiful daughter to become the wife of Swift Arrow, who had looked with favor on Silver Moon for some time. Yellow Dog also believed that the chief's daughter was worthy of his brave grandson and, as time passed, the two chiefs arranged that Swift Arrow should take Silver Moon to his tepee as his wife.

The wish of Silver Moon's father was law among his people, and she must abide by his decisions, but her reluctant promise that she become the bride of Swift Arrow was demanded. She gave her word, but she did not give her heart. In her own camp was a handsome young brave, with whom she had grown up and played since they were old enough to remember. True, he had not had the opportunity to boast of great deeds accomplished on the field of battle, and his father wore no chief's headdress. Neither did he possess great herds of ponies, but this young brave had killed many buffalo, and his tepee was never without plenty of venison. Someday he, too, would be a great hunter and warrior, but now he had only seen twenty Green-Grass-Moons (April). He was brave, and he was handsome, and he had promised to build a white buffalo-skin tepee for Silver Moon when the first wild geese flew north in the spring, and Silver Moon was happy and waiting to share the new white tepee with her lover, Gray Dawn.

But now Gray Dawn's heart was sad. He recently had heard rumors that Oglala Fire had announced that Silver Moon was to be given in marriage to Swift Arrow. He could not understand; he could not believe it true; he wished to see and talk to Silver Moon, but Silver Moon was kept closely watched in her father's tepee and Gray Dawn could get no chance to see her. Day after day he waited and watched, but not once did he see Silver Moon.

Not long after, came the day when Oglala Fire sent the camp crier to announce that the great feast was ready when his daughter was to become the bride of Swift Arrow. The day was to be a day of feasting and dancing. Many of Yellow Dog's warriors came to attend the feast. Swift Arrow was to claim his bride at sunset, just at the time the last rays of sunlight shone on the great gray rock above the camp.

Swift Arrow and his many friends were seen feasting and dancing in their beautiful deerskin costumes. Silver Moon appeared once or twice near the group of dancers, accompanied by her mother and several elder women. She wore her hair tightly plaited in two long braids on either side of her head, and was beautifully robed in a white, tanned-deerskin dress. She did not join in the gaiety of the dance, but soon returned to her father's tepee.

The dancing and feasting continued until late afternoon, when the thoughts of the merrymakers were turning to the approaching event. Swift Arrow had gathered together his closest friends to assist him; all the people were anxiously waiting. At exactly the hour the sun cast its last ray of light on the top of the great gray rock, Swift Arrow and his friends would rush into the great white tepee and bring out the beautiful Silver Moon and claim her as his bride.

The waiting grew intense, as all eyes watched the sun's shadow creep higher and higher on the great stone sentinel, until the single last ray shone on the very top. Then Swift Arrow hastened into the white tepee to bring forth his beautiful bride. All eyes watched the tepee. Soon he reappeared — alone — he called to Oglala Fire, but no one could be found in the tepee. No one understood. Where was Silver Moon?

Then suddenly they heard voices shouting, and Swift Arrow cried, "Look, look, up on the great rock!" and far above them they saw Silver Moon and her lover Gray Dawn, holding each other by the hand while they slowly chanted the death song — and, as the group breathlessly watched, the two lovers, with hands still tightly clasped, leaped to their death, at the last ray of the setting sun.

Chapter XIII

Indian Strategy
AS RELATED BY LONE EAGLE

AS I LOOK BACK OVER THE YEARS OF MY BOYHOOD, I AM REMINDED of a narrative often told to me by Chief Big Elk, my foster father, who roamed the Western plains with old Sitting Bull until the latter's death, in Dakota, in 1890. Well do I remember at the close of the evening meal of cornbread and venison, while Cloud Woman, my foster mother, was arranging the bearskin robes on the earthern floor of our painted tepee, my foster father would take his seat on the ground at the side of the tepee opposite the door flap. Filling his red stone pipe with the cherished kin-ni-kin-nik, he would smoke and gaze out over the open prairie or into the low-burning embers of the evening fire, which told me that he was thinking of the days when the Sioux Indians were monarchs of the great Western plains.

It was at these times that I would edge up close to his side and ask him to tell me of his warrior days when he was a lad like me, and the paleface soldiers had not yet come to build strong houses on the prairies. Many are the interesting and exciting stories he has related to me in the dialect of the Dakotas in that gaily-painted tepee. One incident in particular, which nearly cost his life and the lives of his entire party, was a narrative often related, and one which I well remember.

During the severe winter of 1870-71 the buffalo in the Sioux country had followed the storms toward the west. The Teton and Oglala bands of Sioux then roamed the prairies of the Dakotas west of the Missouri River as far as the Crow and Blackfeet country, in Montana. The following spring, it became necessary to send out scouts toward the west to find out where the buffalo had drifted. To the west were the Crows and Cheyennes, and to the northwest were located the fierce tribe of Blackfeet, all enemies of the Sioux. It took the best Sioux scouts to go through the enemy's country without being seen or trailed.

My foster father, then a young man of about thirty summers, was chosen to lead a party of some twenty Sioux hunters into the Blackfeet country of Montana and look for the buffalo herds. They were all well mounted on Indian ponies and most of them carried sawed-off, muzzle-loading rifles of large bore. They had traveled many days toward the northwest and had encountered several snow squalls, which caused great difficulty in traveling. Being in the early Green Grass Moon (April), the buffalo grass and bunch grass were not sufficiently strong to keep the leg-weary ponies in traveling condition; besides, they had seen no buffalo and their only food consisted of several half-starved pronghorns and an occasional sage hen.

They had traveled as far as the Little Snowy and Bear Paw Mountains, in central Montana, but had not found the main buffalo herds — only a few straggling, half-starved calves and old cows. From a French and Cree half-breed trapper they learned that there were large herds of buffalo on the other side of the Little Snowy mountain range in the Snow Hole, which is now known as the Judith Basin, in Fergus County. As their ponies were nearly exhausted from their long journey through the Badlands and the lack of sufficient food, the party decided to leave their horses and three of their number on the south slope of Black Butte until they returned from their trip into the Judith Basin country. As Black Butte was the highest point in this vicinity, the three hunters could station a scout on top of the pinnacle, who could see plainly all the country for many miles around.

My father and his remaining sixteen hunters started on their perilous journey across the mountains to the Snowy Hole Basin on the western side. Every precaution had to be taken, as they were far into the enemy country of the warlike Black-feet. On the third day of their journey they reached the western slope and began to descend into the beautiful valley below. The foothills emerging into the basin are very rough, composed of high sandstone cliffs with almost perpendicular walls rising a hundred or more feet into the air. The lower rimrocks form a high, rough barrier some fifty to sixty feet high, and nearly as thick, running for many miles along the edge of the basin.

It was this rimrock that obstructed their view of the basin below. And to the back of it, not more than a hundred yards away, were the gigantic cliffs they had been so long in descending, all in plain view of the seemingly imprisoned Sioux hunters in the narrow gorge below. They had heard that there was a narrow, ragged opening some one hundred feet wide, called by the French trappers, "Frenchman's Pass," and known to the Sioux as "Bear Gap," somewhere along the rimrock, but the exact location they did not know. So it was decided to divide the party and go in opposite directions until the gap was located, and the signal given to the remaining party.

My father and his group took the trail toward the north and, after walking a short distance, they came in sight of the pass. They sent a courier to the rest of the party and stepped out on a gravel knoll in the great opening, which gave them a full view of the Judith Basin beyond. What was their great surprise to see, directly in front of them, approaching the gap in single file, a war party of ninety to one hundred Blackfeet warriors all in full war paint, well mounted, and nearly every Indian carrying a rifle, only a few of them being armed with bows and arrows.

The Blackfeet saw the Sioux hunters at practically the same instant. The leader of the mounted war party signaled his men and immediately they spread out over the prairie in a fan shape facing the gap — their chief in the center and slightly in advance of the semicircle. The small party of Sioux hunters was trapped. To escape afoot was impossible. For the mere handful of Sioux to fight the one hundred mounted Blackfeet facing them was certain death. They hastily scanned the narrow canyon and the steep cliffs back of them. They would easily be overtaken by the horsemen if they followed the canyon, and to attempt climbing the jagged cliffs would be very slow work, besides being in easy rifle range of the Blackfeet when they entered the gap.

The knoll or ridge on which they stood was slightly higher than the space between them and the cliff in the rear, and by stepping back a few yards toward the cliff and stooping slightly they would be completely hidden from the view of the war party out on the flats. This small bit of natural formation and the strategic instinct of the Sioux leader were the means of saving the lives of the little party. While the Blackfeet chief and his mounted warriors waited to find, if possible, the exact strength of the Sioux party back of the rimrock walls, all of the Sioux in the gap walked boldly across to the opposite side of the opening, passing out of sight behind the other wall. Then, keeping out of sight of the watchful Blackfeet, they ran back to the slight depression near the cliff and returned in the opposite direction, hidden from view of the valley until they were back of the towering walls on the other side of the gap. Then they would again boldly walk in single file across the knoll in plain view of the amazed Blackfeet; always returning to the opposite side of the gap, hidden from the ever watchful eyes out in the flats.

These seventeen bold Sioux hunters kept up this continuous march past the open gap until the ninety or more mounted warriors out in the valley began to get nervous. After retreating a few paces, the Blackfeet held a hurried council. Still the Sioux kept passing in open sight, occasionally firing a passing shot and giving a yell of defiance to the awe-stricken Blackfeet. A dozen complete marches were made by the Sioux. The Blackfeet had already counted over two hundred Sioux warriors hidden behind the rock walls and still they kept passing down the canyon. One more hurried call of the frightened chief and the entire war party wheeled their mounts and rode away across the prairie out of sight, while the Sioux hunters made their way safely out of the Blackfeet country.

Chapter XIV

An Indian's Dream
AS RELATED BY LONE EAGLE

ON THE WALL OF MY LOG RANCH HOUSE ON EAGLE BAR RANCH, there hangs a beautiful eagle feather Indian war bonnet. This gaily beaded headdress has attracted the attention and admiration of many an Indian and white visitor at the ranch. Many an old Sioux chief has asked the privilege of a close inspection of its rare beauty and workmanship.

This gorgeous and most coveted of all Indian wearing apparel contains thirty-one long and most perfect feathers taken from the tails of the golden eagle, which is the sacred war eagle of the red men. The selected feathers are each about twenty inches long and pure white, with the exception of about six inches of the tip, which is a jet black. They are arranged on a heavily beaded buckskin band, which fits snugly over the forehead allowing the feathers to flow toward the back. This beaded band is fastened to a cap which fits on the head and holds the entire war bonnet in place. The headdress is trimmed with beautifully dyed ermine skins. The material for such a coveted ornament would mean the capture of three eagles and requires some thirty ermine skins. These pelts alone would mean several months of hunting and hardship for the Indian, not counting the difficult task of tanning and making up the material.

Often while sitting near the open fireplace in my room, I have gazed at the array of Indian relics of bygone days which bedeck the walls of the interior. There are beaded moccasins of a dozen different tribes, red stone peace pipes once the sacred property of noted chiefs, tomahawks, bows and arrows, scalping knives, snowshoes, gaily colored blankets, bear-claw necklaces, various designs of beaded buckskin costumes, and even several of the ghastly trophies of the war path — scalps of my foster father's warrior days. But most beautiful and interesting of all is the eagle feather war bonnet. It has an interesting tale to relate and, when I recall the incident, I smile and think of how I became its owner and the price it cost me.

It was many summers ago, and in the Green Corn Moon (August), that my foster father and several of his councilmen received an invitation to visit the Mandan Indians, at their camp on the Cheyenne River, and to participate in the fall council and the four-day Green Corn Dance which was to follow. At my mother's request, it was decided that I could accompany them on their six-day journey to the Mandan country. I was to ride my favorite pony — a pretty black mustang — given to me by Moon Dog, one of my father's closest friends. According to Indian custom I had named the pony after the giver. The trip across the prairie was made on schedule time, and we found the Mandans in full costume awaiting the coming events.

A branch of the Sioux tribe, the Mandans speak nearly the same dialect as the Oglalas, so we had but little difficulty in conversing with our hosts. I became acquainted with several of the Indians of my own age and found them very interesting, but not differing much from the rest of the Dakota tribes. They seemed, however, to take much interest in the fact that I was a paleface with an Indian name, and the adopted son of Chief Big Elk. We became fast friends and talked much of the coming Green Corn Dance. Also they greatly admired Moon Dog.

The Mandans, like all of the western plains tribes, take much pride in their personal appearance and many a beautifully tanned and gaily beaded buckskin costume is worn during their ceremonial dances and special tribal occasions. Among the younger dancers was a chief's son named "Ta-tan-ka Ska" (White Buffalo), and during his part in the dance he wore a most gorgeous war bonnet of golden eagle feathers. Of all the costumes of the various dancers, White Buffalo's war bonnet was the thing that attracted me most. Several times I mentioned the subject of trading or purchasing it from him, but each time my offer was far below his estimation of its value. In fact he showed no desire to dispose of his treasure at all. I had set my mind on owning it if possible, and tried every inducement I could think of, but to no avail.

Finally a new thought came to me. The Mandans are very superstitious, as are all of the pagan Indians. They believe in dreams, and signs of the season and sky. In fact, every Indian's life is strongly guided by his dreams. Even the old-time war parties would not go into battle unless their leader was instructed to do so by a message sent to him from the Great Spirit in a dream, and it was very bad medicine if anyone failed to heed the interpretation of his dream; or even if any of his friends had a dream about him, and he failed to comply with its interpretations. I will admit that, three or four years before, I was a strong believer in all of the Indian superstitions, but during my four years at the reservation mission school I had given up many of the beliefs taught me from my childhood. But, knowing the superstitions of the Mandans, I was fully convinced that White Buffalo was no exception to the rest of his tribesmen.

During that night, as I lay in the big painted tepee of our host, I thought of how proud I would be if I could only return home the possessor of that coveted war bonnet. The following morning, even before the Great Light Maker had peeped at us from over the eastern horizon, I arose and went to White Buffalo's lodge, where I found him preparing his breakfast over a newly kindled fire.

"How, Kola," he greeted me. I returned the greeting in the usual manner. "White Buffalo, my friend," I said, as I motioned him to sit down on a bundle beside me. "I had a most beautiful dream last night, and in this dream I had come all the way from the Oglala country to be your guest; I dreamed we became fast friends, even like brothers, and after I had visited your lodge for many sleeps, it became time for me to return home to my people, but before I departed you gave me your beautiful eagle war bonnet as a token of our great friendship, which pleased me greatly."

White Buffalo dug his moccasined toe into the dirt at his feet and looked troubled. He said nothing, but looked steadily into the fire for several minutes. Finally he arose and walked into the lodge, returning with the war bonnet on his head. Approaching, he bade me stand while he placed it on my head. I returned to our tepee, the proudest boy in all the Mandan village.

We had now been with the Mandans nearly a half moon. The council and the Green Corn Dance were over and we were to return to the Pine Ridge country the following day. On the morning of our departure, all of our pack horses and saddle ponies were rounded up and run into a rope corral by several of the young Mandans. I had just saddled up my own horse and was arranging our bed packs on the herd ponies when White Buffalo approached me with "How Wam-bli Ish-na-la Mita Kola" (Hello, Lone Eagle, my friend). He paused for a few minutes and then continued. "Lone Eagle, I had a most beautiful dream last night, and in my dream you had come from the beautiful country of the Oglalas to visit the Mandan people. I dreamed we became good friends, even like brothers. You stayed with us many sleeps, and when it became time for you to return to your people you gave me a beautiful black pony as a token of our great friendship, which pleased me greatly."

I would rather have given up all my other possessions than to part with Moon Dog, my favorite saddle pony, but to refuse a friend under the prevailing circumstances was an unpardonable breach of Indian etiquette and tribal custom. There was but one thing for me to do. I slowly removed the saddle from

Moon Dog, the choicest of all my possessions, and reluctantly handed the bridle reins to White Buffalo, who led him away out of sight among the Mandan lodges, while, with tear-dimmed eyes, I placed my saddle on one of my father's extra pack horses and accompanied the party back to the Pine Ridge country, a lonesome lad with a much saddened heart. And even yet, when I gaze at the beautiful war bonnet, I often smile and wonder if White Buffalo really did have the vision, which cost me my faithful pony.

Chapter XV

Custer's Last Battle

AUTHENTIC VERSION OF THE CUSTER BATTLE AT THE LITTLE BIG
HORN, AS RELATED BY LONE EAGLE *

IT HARDLY SEEMS POSSIBLE THAT OVER THREE-QUARTERS OF A
century have passed since the famous battle of the Little Big
Horn, which still lives so vividly in the minds of many Indians
and whites in the Northwest. General Custer asked for it, but
it was too bad he had to take so many good men with him.
Custer went out to kill the Sioux, and they killed him instead.

The history of the famous Custer battle, so commonly called
"The Custer Massacre" has been written and rewritten by historians until every American schoolboy has heard of the
"Charge of the Gallant Three Hundred," and yet none of the
histories coincide in detail except as to the fact that not a
man of Custer's troops escaped alive. Hence there was not
one survivor left to tell the tale of that eventful twenty-fifth
day of June, 1876.

Because of the fact that there were no white survivors, it is
evident that the only true story concerning this much misunderstood event would have to be obtained from the Indians
themselves. Since the American Indians are, as a race, very
reticent on matters of this nature and, furthermore, were of

* The particular interest in this story lies in the fact that it is probably the first pres-
entation of the famous Custer Battle from the viewpoint of the Indian rather than
that of the white man.

the opinion that they were regarded as standing enemies of the United States government and would, no doubt, soon all be rounded up as military prisoners, it is no wonder that they hesitated to acknowledge any participation in this battle. I lived all my younger life among the Sioux of the Dakotas and Montana, and knew personally and intimately more than half a hundred Sioux who took part in the battle against Custer's command. I have heard detailed descriptions of the battle

SIOUX VETERANS OF THE CUSTER BATTLE, AT CROW AGENCY, MON-
TANA. PHOTO TAKEN BY LONE EAGLE, JUNE 25, 1926, JUST FIFTY
YEARS AFTER THE BATTLE.

from many different Indians who took the scalps from the Custer slain.

Among the warriors who have given me the most detailed descriptions of every phase of this battle was my foster father, who last rehearsed for me the position of the various groups of men (both Indians and soldiers) on the very site of the battle-field one afternoon in June, 1912. Here he also pointed out to me two markers on the east slope of the knoll where he "counted coup." Another Indian who accompanied us was Curley, who was employed as scout by General Custer at the time of the battle. Curley was a fullblood Crow Indian. I knew Curley and his family well, having lived near him for several years and visited at his ranch many times. He has often told me that he was with Custer's command during the greater part of the battle, but took no actual part. Once or twice he begged Custer to get away or surrender to the Indians, but Custer refused, saying he would rather die fighting than surrender or be taken alive by the Indians. When Curley saw that the soldiers had no chance, he made for cover and wormed his way into a bunch of brush near the bottom of a coulee. He finally gained a position among the Sioux, back of the mounted Indians who were steadily closing in on the soldiers near the crest of the knoll. Curley took no actual part on either side and was in no way molested by the Sioux, who, he stated, must have known he had been with the soldiers at the beginning of the fight.

After the battle, Curley returned to his people and later became a stock raiser and small farmer near the Little Big Horn. He died of pneumonia at his log ranch home on the Crow Reservation only a few years ago at the age of about eighty.

An error often seen, even in history, is that "Chief" Sitting Bull was the head war chief and leader of all the victorious Indians at the battle of the Little Big Horn. This is a gross mistake. Sitting Bull ("Ta-tan ka-eyo-tan-ke"), literally translated "Buffalo-he-sits-down" or "Sitting Buffalo," was a member of the Hun-ka-papa band of Sioux and was a medicine man or high priest and never was considered a war chief. During the Custer fight he was confined close to his tepee in the Hun-ka-papa main camp down on the river, some three miles from the scene of the battle, with a badly crippled leg which he had received the day previous by being kicked by a wounded pack animal.

I never knew Sitting Bull personally, but I knew his widow and young daughter and several relatives who vouched for the above information. One of his nephews, Chauncy Yellow

Robe, was a professor in the government Indian School at Rapid City, South Dakota, until his death a few years ago. His mother was a sister of Sitting Bull.

Sitting Bull was, perhaps, the most written about and the most misunderstood of all our Indians of the West. He was also the most misrepresented by the self-appointed historians and sensational feature writers of that era, whose knowledge of Sitting Bull and the West in general was drawn from hearsay or from pure imagination.

Sitting Bull and Crazy Horse, chief of the Oglalas, were invariably heralded by these sensational feature writers as being the commanders-in-chief of all the Indian warriors at the Little Big Horn. The fact is that Indians in battle never had commanders-in-chief or sub-commanders as in our military system of fighting. Each tribe had various warrior societies of voluntary organizations each with its own head chief and minor chiefs. These chiefs were instructors and advisors in quiet times and never were commanders in time of battle. In battle each individual warrior and each individual warrior chief fought in his own way and not according to orders from any superior. His method of fighting individually from behind rocks, trees, brush, and natural geographic formations, as well as from the back of his swiftly running horse, made him the feared warrior of the plains. It was such warriors who not only outnumbered General Custer at the battle of the Little Big Horn but out-generaled him as well.

Of the five Sioux tribes — the Hun-ka-papas, Oglalas, Minneconjoux, San Arcs, Blackfoot Sioux, and the Cheyennes — represented at the Battle of the Little Big Horn, each had its own chief. Although Sitting Bull, of the Hun-ka-papas, and Crazy Horse, of the Oglalas, were regarded as the two most able chiefs of the alliance, neither had any authority whatsoever outside of his own tribe.

For years, Two Moons also has been heralded as the great war chief of the allied Cheyennes against Custer. Old Cheyenne Indians say that, in 1876, Two Moons was a minor warrior chief, one of twenty-seven minor chiefs then in the tribe. In the fall of 1877, one year after the Custer battle, Two Moons and a small band of Cheyennes surrendered to General Nelson A. Miles at Fort Keogh, Montana, near where Miles City now stands. For Two Moons' quiet and peaceable submission to the general's request, the general "appointed" him a chief, a position never recognized by the Indians themselves. Hence, Two Moons was only a "white-man-made chief," which meant absolutely nothing to the Cheyennes.

Sitting Bull, according to his tribe and all the Indians who knew him, was considered one of the ablest, bravest, and most respected medicine chiefs* of his day. He won disfavor of the local Indian agent and the government only because he would never submit to white man's rule. He steadfastly refused to sign away the tribal lands of his people to the greedy federal land grabbers and was a true and loyal guardian to his trust. Among his people, he was known as a man desiring war only against whiskey traders and the encroaching white man on his hunting grounds. His way of maintaining peace and keeping out of trouble was to remain entirely out of touch with whites and their demoralizing firewater. Sitting Bull never went out of his way looking for trouble, but only wished to be left alone. Nevertheless he was relentlessly hunted and pursued until finally he was shot down under the pretense that he was resisting an arrest by order of white men who were unable to conquer his indomitable spirit.

There are several other facts not generally known concerning this battle: General Custer had no previous meeting with the Indians, and the Indians were not on the move, but had been camped along the Little Big Horn for some time. The camp then comprised the largest body of red warriors ever assembled, and the greatest mobilization of Indian might this continent ever saw — not less than 1,800 tepees and over 5,500 people, of which at least 3,500 were fighting warriors.

Most of the warriors were mounted and had about an equal number of bows and guns. The guns comprised a mixture of

---

* A "medicine chief" or peace-time chief was not considered a war chief.—Ed.

shell and percussion-cap rifles, the best of which were the modern 1873 Winchester .44 calibre repeating rifles. Many of the older guns were discarded or turned over to the younger braves after the Indians gained possession of Custer's Springfield carbines and Colt revolvers. Most of these captured guns were retaken from the Indians by the United States Government at the time of the so-called Battle of Wounded Knee. A few of these old Custer carbines and revolvers are still owned by the Sioux.

On my ranch in central Montana I still have a Colt revolver, a Springfield carbine, several brass uniform buttons, a pair of saddle bags, and a scalp lock which was taken from the battlefield by my foster father.

There was at least one woman warrior among the Indians who took an active part in the battle against Custer and his men. She was One-Who-Walks-With-the-Stars, a young woman of the Oglala tribe and the wife of Crow Dog. Crow Dog rode out with others of his band to meet Custer while his wife went up the river to locate several of their horses which had strayed away from their bunch on the Greasy Grass flats above. Not being able to locate them right away, she followed the west side of the stream for some distance, when suddenly she saw a hatless trooper running down a ravine toward the river on the opposite side. She ran behind some trees nearby and watched him plunge into the swift current and make for the shore, near where she was hiding. He was having considerable trouble against the whirling current and was slowly being carried downstream to a bend in the river, where the ascending bank was steep and the water deep. He managed, however, to get a foothold at the base of the slippery bank, and was momentarily compelled to hold on there, shoulder deep in the swift water.

One-Who-Walks-With-the-Stars picked up a club nearby and with the aid of a knife in her belt, she slashed and beat him over the head until he was forced to let go and she never saw him above water again. While still scanning the waters below for the soldier she had just encountered, she heard yelling across the stream and looked up to see another trooper running down the ravine closely followed by a mounted warrior brandishing a war club and gaining rapidly on the man afoot. The trooper had a long gun in his hand and ran into the river up to his waist, when, she said, he threw it far out into the current and started floundering and swimming for the opposite shore. The current was fairly swift at this place and the swimmer was being carried downstream at a rapid rate. The mounted warrior did not ride into the water but stayed on the opposite bank and slowly followed the trooper down the stream. When One-Who-Walks-With-the-Stars saw him endeavoring to make for the shore nearest her, she ran down to the edge of the water and, still wielding her club and knife, she waded out to about waist deep and began beating and slashing at the floundering swimmer. He turned completely around several times in the water and then started back again for mid-stream, but apparently never made it across, as she followed downstream for some distance but never saw him again. Therefore at least two of Custer's troopers succeeded in escaping from the ranks of the Seventh on the fated hill only to be caught later and slain by a woman warrior.

Crow Dog, husband of One-Who-Walks-With-the-Stars, also relates his personal experience that day on the battlefield. When he left his camp to ride out with the others, he heard guns firing in the distance across the river. At first he did not see any soldiers, nor did he know where they were, who they were, or how many there might be. He saw many warriors afoot and on horseback yelling and running up the hill across the river from his camp. He followed for some distance in a wide circle up several ravines and when he got to the top of a small hill he saw many soldiers, and the Indians gradually encircling them from all sides. "Everybody was fighting and yelling, and soon the noise and dust and smoke was so heavy you could not see or hear anything that anyone was yelling. I rode around the soldiers in a circle and saw many loose horses. I caught three soldier horses and hurried with them to my lodge across the river, but when I got back I did not see any more horses and every soldier man was killed."

One statement that may be of interest is that not all of Custer's troops and civilian attaches were scalped as is often stated in historical writings. Old warriors state that probably one-half of Custer's men were left on the battlefield with their scalps on. Some near the river, where they had tried to make their escape through the Sioux lines, were found afterwards by the women of the camp and were mutilated in revenge for their unprovoked attack on a camp containing old men, women, and children. This was, in no sense of the word, a war party and had no intention of participating in any attack, as Sioux war parties were never accompanied by their women and children.

Custer's body was stripped of its clothing, but he was not scalped. His sorrel horse was captured by a young Sioux and ridden by him on many a buffalo hunt in after years. Comanche, Captain Keogh's mount, was found wounded near the battlefield two days later by the soldiers who came to bury the soldier dead. He recovered from his wounds and was taken to old Fort Lincoln, where he was retired and never ridden again, but was always led with an empty saddle in all parade formations at the old fort, until he died at the advanced age of twenty-eight.

General Custer did not have long, curly red hair as he is so often pictured in paintings and sketches. It is true that during his career as a Civil War officer, he did dress somewhat as a dandy, with long, flowing locks, in Buffalo Bill frontier style. But, just previous to his Indian campaign, a general War Department order was issued which caused him to cut his hair quite short, in which style it remained up to the day of his death.

During the commencement exercise of 1924, at West Point Military Academy, I had the pleasure of personally meeting Mrs. George A. Custer, who, at that time, made her home in New York City. With her I visited the monumental tomb of her husband at West Point, where he is now buried. She related to me the above facts concerning his personal appearance at the time she bade him farewell for the last time at Fort A. Lincoln, Dakota territory, a few days before the battle.

Here we also correct another error which so often misguides the reader concerning the military rank of Custer during his campaign against the Sioux. True, George A. Custer ("The Boy General") did hold the rank of brigadier general during some of his Civil War days but, owing to his repeated habit of disobeying orders from his superiors, he had placed himself in a bad light with the War Department in Washington and had been demoted to the rank of lieutenant colonel, which title he held at the time of his Indian campaign in the West.

On the Custer battlefield in Montana, there are small white granite markers placed, presumably, at the exact spot where every soldier fell, bearing the name of the fallen fighter, but the slain troopers were buried in the Custer Battlefield Cemetery, farther down the slope and below the large monumental shaft which is inscribed with the names of the 230 or more dead. All the troopers except Custer and a few of his commissioned officers lie buried in this cemetery.

Another question often asked in connection with this battle is: How many Indians were killed and what became of the dead warriors? None was ever found on the hill among Custer's men when Reno* came to bury the soldier dead two days after the battle. There were about thirty Sioux warriors killed during the battle on that day, and the Sioux dead were all left in abandoned tepees along the river.

Some years ago, while on a visit to my old home on the Pine Ridge Reservation, I spent some time at the ranch home of an old warrior friend, Spotted Rabbit, veteran of the Little Big Horn. Living in his home at the time was his uncle, Ta-tan-ka Ska (White Buffalo), then about eighty years old, also a veteran of the Custer battle. White Buffalo was a sort of historian of his tribe, and it was from him that I learned the names of the Sioux warriors killed by Custer's troops. The names on the original deerskin are sketched in Sioux picture writing

* Reno was a major under Custer but he did not participate in the battle.

and are the Oglala Dakota (Sioux) names. I have given a literal English translation to these twenty-nine names and, as far as I know, this complete list has never been known outside the Sioux nation and has never before been published: Deeds, Black Fox, Bear-With-Horn, Bad-Light-Hair, Chased-By-Owls, Cloud Man, Dog-With-Horns, Dog's-Back-Bone, Elk Bear, Flying By, Guts (or Open Belly), Hawk Man, Kills Him, Lone Dog, Long Robe, Left-Handed-Ice, Mustache, Owns-Red-Horse, Plenty Lice, Red Face, Swift Bear, Standing Elk, Swift Cloud, Three Bears, White Eagle, White-Buffalo-Bull, Young Bear, Young Skunk, and Young-Black-Moon. Several others were, of course, wounded and crippled. One died of his wounds a few days later, while on their hurried move to Canada, which would bring the total number of Sioux dead up to thirty.

Lone Bear, a Cheyenne from the Northern Cheyenne Reservation, in Montana, gave the number of Cheyenne warriors killed as six, namely: Black Bear, Hump Nose, Lame-White-Man, Limber Bones, Noisy Walking, and Whirl Wind. They were all buried in the hills west of their camp on the Little Big Horn, in the crevices along the rimrocks. Remnants of these burials could be seen as late as 1916. I believe they have all been destroyed by now.

One Cheyenne warrior also died from his wounds some days later, making a total of seven dead among the Cheyennes, or a grand total of thirty-seven lost by the combined Indian forces against Custer.

Another interesting incident in connection with Custer's last march, was related to me by Mato-Sapa-Najene (Standing-Black-Bear), who, with two other young Dakotas named Deeds and Brown Back, were sent out on an early morning scouting trip to the hills toward the east of the upper Sioux camp. They had ridden for some time when they crossed Custer's pack trail and, following it for some distance, they found a box of hard-tack which had been lost from the pack train. They broke open the box and began eating, while Standing-Black-Bear stood near filling his warbag with the bread. It is supposed that one of the troopers missed the lost pack and was returning over the trail looking for it when he saw one of the Indians. The trooper shot and killed Deeds instantly.

Standing-Black-Bear and Brown Back, seeing that Deeds was dead, and not knowing how many more soldiers might be in the party, hastily mounted their ponies and made a dash for the nearest coulee. Following the low ravines, they returned to their camp with the news. Deeds was, no doubt, the first casualty of the day, even though he was killed miles away from the scene of the battle, and some hours before Custer's troops met their end.

Many students of American history have been told that the battle lasted all day on that hot and dusty Sunday. The truth is that the fight lasted less than two hours from the time Custer's bugler sounded "dismount" at about 11:30 A. M. The Indians were camped along the Little Big Horn River, their villages extending along the valley, or bottom lands, for some three miles. The Indian scouts had known of the presence of soldiers since they first crossed the Yellowstone, but evidently did not think that they were coming to the Little Big Horn. If so, they did not count on their arrival so soon, as no preparations were being made for any kind of encounter. Men, women, and children were completing their routine morning camp work casually. Some of the women were washing along the river banks. Their ponies were still peacefully grazing up on the benchlands, a mile or more from the villages. Only a few of the younger men had gone out and driven in small bunches of the horses, which were leisurely drinking along the stream. As soon as the warning was given that soldiers were in the vicinity, the warriors and young men hurried out on the benchlands, rounded up all their ponies, and went out to meet the soldiers about two miles above the village.

Custer was, unknowingly, advancing toward the main camp when met by the Indians. As soon as he saw the mass of mounted warriors advancing toward him from three sides, and saw, after a few minutes, that his retreat was cut off, he gave orders to dismount, at which call one man from each squad was assigned to care for the troop horses. Here it was that Custer made his worst blunder, an unwise decision in his position and circumstances, that surprised even the Indians. No sooner had the soldiers dismounted than the Indians stampeded all the horses and pack animals and soon were in possession of hundreds of cases of government ammunition, which they much needed and which left the troopers with but a few rounds of ammunition before the first half hour of fighting was over.

The mounted warriors completely encircled Custer's troops and began firing as soon as they came in range. The shooting was heavy at first but grew steadily less as many of Custer's men fell out of the fighting. Hundreds of Indians were riding around the soldiers as they hastily formed little groups on the side of the hill. Both mounted warriors and Indians afoot steadily closed in, as Custer's men became fewer and fewer.

General Custer and his brother, Captain Tom Custer, were among the last score or so of men to be seen assembled in a small group near the top of the hill. They were still fighting, and endeavoring to make each bullet count, as it was evident that they were nearing their last round. As the firing on both sides became more and more interrupted, some of the Indians called out to the soldier chief to surrender.

Here it might be stated that, up to this point, very few, if any, of the Indians knew what troops they were fighting or who the white soldier chief was. Very few of the Sioux had ever seen Custer and not many knew him by sight. To those few who had seen or knew him, he was known as White Soldier Chief "Long Hair," because of his custom of wearing his auburn hair very long and since he did not have long hair at this time, he was not readily recognized as "Long Hair" even after he was dead. Rain-in-the-Face was one of the first to recognize him definitely after the battle, because Custer and his brother Tom had once had him under military arrest for several months, up in the Dakotas, some years earlier.

The true facts concerning the last few minutes of fighting

were told to me on several different occasions by not less than
a half-dozen Sioux who saw it in detail and at close range.
Custer, so far as is known, was never hit by any of the Indian
bullets or arrows until all but eighteen or twenty of the soldiers were out of the fighting. Then he was seen to grab at his
side or hip and fall in a kneeling position, and within a few
minutes he fell or stretched out on the ground with his face
on his forearm. Many Indians were now yelling to their braves
to cease firing. No one knew who fired the shot that struck him
in the side. Rain-in-the-Face often made the claim that he shot
both the general and his brother, for whom he had a personal
grudge, but the Indians say that because of the noise, dust,
smoke, and confusion, no one knew. I knew Rain-in-the-Face
very well and have seen him and talked with him many times
at his home in the Dakotas and again only a short time before
his death, in 1908. He always declared that he recognized and
shot both the Custers, but I never found anyone who could
verify the statement.

The Indians continued firing on the soldiers at intervals
and, in many instances as the troopers' ammunition gave out,
the warriors rode up and hit them over the head with their
war clubs or guns to finish them. Also, many were seen to use
their last bullets on themselves — a lost soldier's "coup de
grace." Spotted Rabbit, one of the half-dozen Sioux who gave
me the details of the battle, and Big Elk, my foster father,
were two of a small group who were nearest Custer. While
they were advancing with caution, a young warrior who had
lost his brother in the fight, became so enraged at the soldiers
that he rushed in among the small group and, before anyone
realized what he intended to do, he fired point-blank at the
fallen general as he lay wounded on the ground, sending another bullet into his left side a few inches above the first one.
At this deed of cowardice even the Indians were enraged at
the young warrior and eventually disowned him as a member of their tribe. He was forced to live apart from his people
in dugouts and old castaway tents, never being allowed to par-

ticipate in any tribal festivities. Some years later he died, a hermit, on the Dakota Reservation.

Whether either of the two wounds received by General Custer would have proved fatal no one can say. However, it is known among the Sioux that he rallied and fainted by spells as the Indians cautiously proceeded toward him. The general, gaining a sitting or reclining position, waved them back. While the warriors were grouped not far away watching him, and before any of them caught the significance of the moment, the wounded general took his revolver from its holster and, placing the gun to his head, fired the shot that ended the life of the soldier chief who, possibly, might have survived the most famous battle in all our western American history. It is my belief and also the belief of many of the Indians that Custer feared a final torture at the hands of his enemies, but I am convinced that they would have spared his life, as they held the greatest respect for a brave man, although he may have been their enemy. Also, many officers and even the tribal chiefs believed that Custer had a chance of becoming the next President, and it was their sincere belief that he would treat them well.

In June, 1926, during the fiftieth anniversary of the battle at the Little Big Horn, I revisited the scene of the fight in company with such nationally known men as General E. S. Godfrey, William S. Hart, D. F. Barry, Chiefs Standing Bear and Joe Red Cloud, of the Sioux; White-Man-Runs-Him; Chief Plenty Coups, of the Crows; Chief Two Moons, of the Cheyennes; Red Tomahawk, the Indian mounted policeman who killed Sitting Bull during the Ghost Dance in Dakota in 1890; a few veterans of both the Reno and Bentine troops; and several Sioux and Cheyenne veterans as guides. We reviewed the Custer battle and heard for the last time, no doubt, a brief outline of the famous fight of just fifty years before. The same evening all the chiefs and aged veterans of the Sioux held their last council fire together and, during this very impressive ceremony, they proclaimed their great warrior, Chief

Crazy Horse, as being the greatest Indian that ever lived. They then bestowed upon William S. Hart, renowned western screen actor and friend of the Sioux, the honored name of "Ta-sunka Witko" (Crazy Horse), in whose honor they made him an adopted member of the Sioux nation. It was my great pleasure to sit in witness of this grand council and welcome the last white man ever to be adopted by the veteran warriors and red monarchs of the Western plains.

In closing this story of Custer's last stand, I wish to state in behalf of my Sioux brothers that practically all of the past hatred and hostility on our Western frontier was due to a gross misunderstanding of the American Indian, who was defending his hunting grounds and his home fires from a stronger and superior invading race.

HENRY STANDING BEAR (AGE 13) UPON HIS ARRIVAL AT THE
CARLISLE INDIAN SCHOOL, OCTOBER 6, 1880.

Chapter XVI

Last Chief of the Oglalas

AS RELATED BY LONE EAGLE

WHEN WORD WAS BROUGHT BACK TO THE PINE RIDGE RESERVA-
tion that the Sioux had completely wiped out the command
of Long Hair on the Little Big Horn, Totola was but nine
years old. He had never seen a white man. Buffalo still roamed
the Black Hills and Dakota prairies in vast herds.

The Sioux were great hunters and warriors; they ruled all
the vast country between the Big Sioux River and the Yellowstone. Crazy Horse, Hollow-Horn-Bear, Spotted Tail, and
Standing Bear, his father, had often told their people that this
vast domain of the Dakotas would always remain the hunting
grounds of the Sioux. So this young warrior grew up in the
belief that his people would always be sole rulers of the greatest buffalo herds in the West, but he did not understand the
white man's greed for gold and the rich prairie lands of the
Sioux. He had always had dreams of someday being a great
hunter and brave warrior like all his ancestors before him,
but his hopes and dreams were never to be realized.

When the warriors of his tribe returned from the hunt and
the warpath, he would sit around the campfire and listen to
his elders tell of their great deeds of valor, and he dreamed and
waited for the day when he, too, would be able to relate his
adventures to many eager listeners. With his bow and arrows
he became the best hunter among the younger boys. His elders

taught him to follow trails through the mountains and over wide prairies, where, to the casual observer, there was not a visible sign of wild animal or foe. He learned to put on his war paint and dance and sing the rhythmic chants of the Sioux. He learned all the things that a successful hunter and warrior should know.

By the time he was thirteen, he was ready to go with his elders on buffalo-hunting trips and on the war trails. He had now outgrown his childhood and had won the right to a new and more honorable name. The elder wise men of his tribe proclaimed he would, from this time on, be called "Mato Najin" (Young Standing Bear), in honor of his father, Standing Bear, the elder, a great warrior and wise councilman of his tribe.

But here again, unusual events and circumstances were to play a part in his life which would change his entire future into a path of which he never dreamed. The buffalo were, by this time, being swiftly driven off the prairies and wantonly slaughtered by the growing numbers of white hunters, just for the hides and for sport. Treaties were being broken by the greedy white men for the gold in the fabulously rich Black Hills, which had been given to the Sioux many years before. Also rich prairie lands of the Oglalas were being thrown open to the white settlers — lands that were promised to the Indians of the Dakotas. They could now plainly see that to fight a far more numerous and superior force would spell only doom to the Indian, although he be the rightful owner of his ancestral home. Old warriors and council tribesmen could see that their only chance of survival would be to understand the ways of the white man and meet him on legal grounds instead of on the warpath. Young people of the tribe must go to school and learn the white man's ways and then some day be able to have an understanding of their problems.

And thus it was that Young Standing Bear was chosen, among others of his tribe, to leave his tepee home and the carefree life of the Dakota Indian camps and attend a school hundreds of miles away from his people and friends. He arrived in Carlisle, Pennsylvania, still garbed in blanket, beaded buckskins, waist-length braided hair, and face paints, in the second year of the Carlisle Indian School, in 1880, when he was thirteen years old. Eight years later he was graduated with honors never having been permitted to visit his boyhood home during the entire time.

Soon after his return to his people, Henry Standing Bear was chosen chief of the numerous Oglala Sioux. He became active in tribal affairs and later was acclaimed chief of all chiefs of the Plains Indians. He was, without question, one of the greatest orators of his race, and was regarded as the foremost leader in the annals of the chiefs' council and the greatest chief of his people in our modern times.

BEFORE THE WHITE MAN CAME

Many suns had kissed the morning,
Many moons adorned the night,
Come and gone full many winters
And as many summers bright.
The while across the broad prairies,
Through the forests deep and still,
O'er the plains and up the mountains
Roamed the red man at his will.
Warrior, chieftains, men of fame,
Long before the white man came.

'Neath the pine tree's friendly shadows,
On the shore of lake or stream,
Here he pitched his humble wigwam,
Near the water's crystal gleam;
And swan-like glide across the water,
In his light birch-bark canoe,
Lived in harmony with nature
And his great god, Manitou,
Catching fish and trapping game,
Long before the white man came.

Reared he here his sons and daughters,
Nature's children plain and free,
Temperate, moral, true, and honest,
He knew no law but liberty.
Bound by no confederation,
Scarcely knowing of its worth,
Yet the Indians were the sovereigns
Of the greatest land on earth.
Possession being their sovereign claim,
Long before the white man came.

He heard the voice of the "Great Spirit"
In the thunder's rumbling sound,
While whispering winds brought him a message
From the Happy Hunting Ground.
By suns and moons and winters
Counted he the days and months and years,
And in the mystic sky-blue waters
Read he all his hopes and fears.
Read destiny in drops of rain,
Long before the white man came.

Thus they dwelt for generations
In their own dear native land,
From sea to sea an earthly Eden,
With fish and game at every hand;
Countless birds sang in the forest,
Anthems rang from all the trees,
And the wild flowers in profusion
Scented every wind and breeze.
Paradise, or much the same,
Long before the white man came.

Chapter XVII

My Boyhood Days Among the Sioux
AS RELATED BY LONE EAGLE

IN LOOKING BACK OVER THE YEARS THAT I LIVED AMONG THE Oglala Sioux, I recall many incidents and happenings of the carefree life in the noisy Indian camps that contrast, in many ways, with my later life with my brother in this modern civilization. The education and training of the Indian boy or girl is just as important to his future way of living as our school or college is to the paleface young man or woman. The young Indian was taught the things that meant his livelihood and success in his tepee home and on the warpath. In the old days, the training of the boy began at the age of five or six. His father fashioned out a bow and arrows for his young son, and often the grandfather was his teacher, gray hairs and long experience being more important and revered than youth. The grandfather tells him many stories of the hunt and the warpath. He hears the thrilling tales of the braves of his tribe. He shoots his first bird or small animal, and is praised for it. It becomes the topic of many evening talks around the family fireside. He feels that he has become important to his family.

Then there are foot racing and horse racing, ball playing, bird hunting, deer hunting, and, in the olden days, the whole village went on the buffalo chase. All this was education for him. These were the schools in which the Sioux boy was educated. What the father or grandfather does he will do; what his father knows he will know; the Indian boy is a good imitator; he needs only the example and praise of a brave warrior or a good hunter and he strives to be like him or excel if possible.

Sioux children are whipped rarely, they are petted and indulged a good deal, but not more than children in paleface families. With few exceptions, they grow up affectionate and kind, the pride of father and mother. The love and understanding of parents have accomplished this, and the children revere and respect their elders more than do many of their more civilized paleface neighbors.

In the long winter evenings, while the fire is burning bright in the center of the lodge and the men are gathered to smoke, he hears the folklore and legends of his people from the lips of the older men. He learns to sing the love songs and war songs of generations gone by. He learns to hold up the sacred red stone pipe to the Great Spirit of his people. As he grows older, he becomes a successful hunter and a great warrior, and what he does not know is not worth knowing for a Dakota. His education is finished and, if he has not already done so, he can now demand the hand of one of the beautiful maidens of the village.

The early-day custom of marriage among the plains tribes was picturesque and most romantic. The Dakota boy sees a young maiden he would like for his own. If she is out carrying water or gathering wood or buffalo chips for the tepee fire, he will meet her and assist her in her work. He may walk along home with her and, if their friendship should prove mutual, he might call on her at her mother's tepee during the evening, and serenade her with a "co-tan-ka" (flute) made from an eagle's wing bone. When the time comes that he decides to claim her hand, he and his parents or friends make up a present to the girl's father. This could be large or small, according to the wealth of the suitor or his family, and may be anything from a gaily colored blanket to many horses.

This present, or "wo-hapa-pi" — which, literally, means bundle of purchase — is taken to the tepee door of the girl's father. If he moves or takes possession of the present within four days, he gives his approval of the young man. However, if this is not satisfactory, either because of the small amount or the character of the young man, the wo-hapa-pi is left undisturbed and the young man is rejected by the father. Sometimes, however, the young couple decides to elope and in most cases, this action is forgiven as the moons roll by. If the young man's offer is accepted by the girl's father, the suitor may claim his sweetheart personally or may send some close friend or relative to bring her to his tepee. This constitutes the full tribal marriage ceremony and thus begins a new family in the Sioux village. Very rarely is such a marriage vow broken.

In the olden days, it was customary for the new son-in-law never to speak to his wife's mother. If they saw each other at a distance, one of them veered from the path until the other passed by. However, they were considered good friends at all times and, should either one wish to convey any word to the other, someone other than the immediate families would gladly carry the message. They never entered the same tepee at the same time although the mother could visit her daughter at any time she chose, when her son-in-law was absent.

There is no exact equivalent in the Sioux language for the word "home" as we know it. The word "tepee" means house or living place. The buffalo-hide tepee was sole property of the Dakota wife. She dressed and tanned the skins; she put up the tepee and took it down and tied it on her pony's back when she was on the trail. But when the gaily painted tepee was pitched and the dry grass, bearskins, and robes were in place, her warrior took the place of honor, which was the back part opposite the door. The wife's place was on his right — or on the left side as one entered the door. The children came in between the mother and the father. The grandmother or aunt had the corner by the door, opposite the woman of the house. If the man had more than one wife, they had separate tepees or arranged to occupy different sides of one. The back part of the tepee, the most honorable place and the one usually occupied by the father, was extended to an honored guest while visiting the family.

The picturesque tepee of the plains tribes was practical and comfortable in any weather. The making of the tepee was done solely by the women. When enough skins were procured by her husband, she sewed them together in a size and pattern to meet the needs of her family. A twenty-foot tepee required a total area of skins some twenty by forty feet square. By means of a twenty-foot rope or leather string, she marked out a half circle and cut the circular side. This gave her a cone-shaped covering some twenty feet high and twenty feet in diameter. The best-designed tepee was always a couple of feet more in diameter than its height. The smoke flaps at the top were arranged in such a way as to draw out the smoke by proper arrangement with the prevailing wind. It could also be arranged to keep out the rains in stormy weather.

The customary way for the wife to set up her tepee was to erect a tripod of three poles of proper length which had been tied together near the smaller ends before being raised. The larger ends were placed in a previously marked circle on the ground. She then set up eleven or twelve more poles evenly distributed around the tripod in a circle. These poles were then securely tied together by simply walking around the entire circle of poles wrapping them with rope. The tepee cover was then lifted up to the top of the conical pole frame by means of another pole tied to the proper place on the cover. Then it was necessary only to bring each side of the cover around to the front, where it was pinned or skewered together by small wooden sticks, some six to eight inches long. Stakes were driven in the ground to hold the cover firmly down in place.

The door opening always faced the east. The inside often was lined part way up by a second piece of hide to keep the draft off persons sitting inside. Many skins and robes were placed on the floor. A hole some two feet square was dug in the center of the tepee for the fire, which was used for warmth and cooking. By proper manipulation of the sides and smoke flaps, the smoke could be held in the top of the tepee above the family and serve as a mosquito protection in the spring. The family all slept in a circle with their heads away from the fire. Mats were made of reeds tied with long rawhide strings. These mats were some six to seven feet long by three feet wide, making a sort of hammock bed and day seat, which was fastened at the back or upper end by long sticks driven in the ground and adjusted to suit. I lived for many years in these Indian tepees and found them very spacious and comfortable in all seasons of the year. Colds or sickness among tepee dwellers were very rare.

I once had an experience which well illustrated the fact that the family tepee belonged to the woman of the home and that she was the undisputed owner and guardian of its safety. The day of the Sun Dance ceremony had arrived and hundreds of Indians were coming into the encampment from every part of the reservation, by wagons, and horseback and travois. My foster mother, Cloud Woman, had put up our tepee early that morning and we were settled for the gala occasion. Next to our camp, several families had stopped and were putting up their lodges. The menfolks were caring for the teams, and a very elderly grandmother was unwrapping a large tepee cover in preparation to putting it up on the tepee frame. She finally succeeded in getting the cover up to its proper place and was trying to bring the sides around in front when a strong gust of wind came up and jerked her off her feet. The wind was whipping the old Indian granny and the loose cover in circles all around the tepee poles. I could see that the little eighty-year-old lady was slowly getting the worst of the deal, so I rushed over and grabbed the wildly flapping cover just as she was lifted completely off her feet and waved roughly in the now husky breeze. When she saw I was helping her, her pride was hurt because I believed she would need my help then, or any other time. She chased me a dozen yards and gave me a sound scolding for belittling her prowess. To show her hurt pride further, she pulled the canvas cover completely off and then proceeded to tear down the fourteen-pole tepee frame, tied it behind her saddle pony and dragged it all over to a new location, fully a half block away, where she began putting it up all over again. When I strolled by her camp a half hour later, her tepee was completely set up and she was sitting in the doorway. As I passed, she turned her back on me to show her contempt of one who did not think her capable of putting up her own castle, alone and unassisted.

The old buffalo-skin tepees are seen no more. The Indian women have had to replace the buffalo covering with canvas, purchased at the white man's store, but the picturesque and age-old style still remains the same. The woman of the house still insists on designing and owning her own shelter, and sets it up and takes it down alone as did her great-grandmother a hundred years ago.

The wanton destruction of the vast herds of buffalo by the white man spelled the doom of the free life of our plains Indian. The buffalo furnished him with all that he needed for a happy and plentiful existence; with his wild herds on the great plains his was a completely self-sustaining nation. I have known many hunters who have seen great herds cross the Missouri and Yellowstone rivers; herds that took two and three days to pass a given point, and some of which were more than a mile wide. Conservative white men and Indians alike have estimated these vast herds at from two million to three million each. A conservative estimate would place our Western buffalo at from fifty to sixty million when Lewis and Clark crossed the plains in 1804.

The American bison is the only living animal that faces a storm instead of turning face away from it. His shaggy head and shoulders furnish the greatest protection against a blizzard of any native American animal known. In the olden days, the Dakota people did not have horses. Big Elk often told me that his people once traveled on foot when on the march or hunting game. He told me of how the grandfather of his grandfather hunted buffalo with only his bows and arrows, and used the old-time natural buffalo traps to get much of the winter's supply of meat for the tribe. The Indians would locate a natural high cliff somewhere near a large herd of feeding buffalo, and pitch their tepees in two rows in a fan shape or V shape extending out on the prairie with the apex or small end of the two rows leading up to the edge of the cliff, forming a funnel. All the old men, and the women and children would be lined up near the rows of tepees. Then the hunters and dogs would drive a herd of the grazing buffalo into the open or wide end of the funnel, with the old men, women, and children yelling to keep the animals between the two lines, which narrowed and led up to the cliff. The frightened and madly running buffalo would plunge or be pushed off the steep cliff by the hundreds, and the Indians would have only to go down in the canyon below and club or shoot the fallen animals. A successful drive would supply meat enough for many an Indian family. This method of trapping buffalo often was used in more recent years by many of the plains tribes long after the horse came into common use.

My foster father told me that, when his father was a young man, his tribe went on such a buffalo hunt in the Black Hills. A large camp was moving into the Hills country for the fall buffalo hunt. The scouts had reported a large herd of buffalo some distance ahead of the moving tribe, so the mounted hunters rode on to overtake the herd before the rest of the band came up to prepare the meat. Not all of the Indians had horses in those days, so the ones that were mounted did the hunting, while the ones afoot cared for the meat. The families who did not own horses used dogs to carry their small children and tepee equipment. The younger children were strapped to a dog's back or sides in a sort of harness. It so happened that his aunt had placed her small baby on the dog's back while on the long march across the plains. When the hunters rode out ahead to the buffalo herd, several of the dogs became unmanageable and ran after the mounted horses. Among the barking dogs wildly chasing the galloping hunters was his aunt's dog with the small Indian baby strapped on his back. Their calls were of no avail and the riders did not know the dogs were following. It was some hours before the dog was found, and when, at last, he was located, the baby was missing from the tired dog's back. Many searchers scoured the tall grass and canyons for miles around, but the baby was never seen again.

I made a trip over nearly the same old hunting grounds when I was living with Big Elk's family in the White River country. Some fifty or sixty families were enroute to attend the annual Sun Dance on Wounded Knee Creek. I was perhaps fourteen or fifteen years old and was the proud possessor of a little black pony of my own, which was a recent gift of my father and had been ridden but a short time. We would be on the trail some two sleeps. In our family group was "An-pe Win" (Day Woman), young wife of "Wanmdi Okiye" (One-who-talks-with-the-Eagle). She had her small baby neatly wrapped in the "I-yo-ko-pa" (cradle), in which they carried their small children and which allowed them to sleep or be carried anywhere. An-pe Win had only one pony for her travois and all her tepee and household equipment, so as I wanted to be helpful to one of our family group on the trail, I offered to carry the baby cradle. I hung the beautifully beaded cradle on the horn of my saddle while the little fellow slept on, but his peaceful slumber was not to last for long. My pony was quite gentle under the saddle but the cradle board was new to him. Wishing to keep up with some of my companions, I put the pony into a slow gallop. The cradle slapped him on the shoulder a couple of times, which apparently was not to his liking, as he immediately bogged his head and began trying to rid himself of his annoyance. He got rid of me in the first half dozen pitches, but the baby, in his rawhide cradle was quite securely tied on to the saddle. I landed on my skypiece somewhat ahead of my bucking pony, who kept right on pitching and swinging the baby and his cradle all over the saddle like a ham on a hook. The little pony was almost at the point of exhaustion when the cradle strap finally broke and let loose the now yelling young warrior. Young War Eagle, cradle and all, landed in a heap yards ahead of the nearest group of mounted Indians, who had given chase to my frightened pony soon after I was thrown from my saddle. The young Indian was but little worse off for his experience, and outside of a few scratches and a bumped nose, he came out of the affray much better than I did. Day Woman did not hesitate to express her opinion of me and my pony as a touring perambulator, and carried her own young War Eagle during the rest of the trip.

After our arrival at the camp on Wounded Knee Creek, many of the Indian women went down below the camp to do their washing. Several of them had taken their small babies with them and placed the cradles near the water so that they could be watched while the mother did her washing. Several of us boys were playing in the vicinity of the creek and, while engaged in our game of hunter and deer, I noticed one of the babies crying, so stopped to amuse him for a moment. His cradle board was hanging on a cottonwood tree near the bank overlooking the Indian women below. The mother had moved up the creek a short way and was temporarily out of sight of her young son.

Thinking this was the cause of his loneliness, I took the cradle down from the tree and carried it up on the edge of the bank some thirty or forty feet above where his mother was, and as soon as he caught sight of her the tears turned to smiles. I propped the cradle board up against some greasewood brush on the edge of the forty-foot sloping gravel bank and went on with my play with the rest of the boys. However, something must have slipped or a gentle breeze blew the bush and tipped the cradle board too far forward, as the first thing I knew that beautiful beaded cradle and contents came tumbling and sliding down the gravel bank, carrying a cloud of dust and gravel along with it. When the dust had cleared away the young warrior was located at the bottom with a big smile on his dusky face, and not even a scratch. He evidently thought the grand slide was arranged especially for his delight and benefit. However, the Indian women did not think too well of this rough way of amusing their young warriors and I had completely lost all my prestige as the camp's champion baby sitter.

The horse was perhaps the most useful of all the Indians' possessions. The oldest Indians say that the plains Sioux came into first possession of horses about 1750, when they procured them by trade or raids on tribes in the Southwest. The Comanche and Apache tribes acquired them from the early Spaniards. The records of Lewis and Clark, during their westward journey through the Sioux country, in 1804, state that the Indians told them that the plains Indians of the Northwest had been using horses only about fifty years. Many horses escaped from their owners in the early days on the plains and, consequently, many bands of wild horses roamed over the sparsely settled areas of the West. The Indians acquired many good horses from these wild herds.

There were several ways of capturing these wild horses. One often used was to locate a small bunch of ten or fifteen horses and, using about the same number of riders, we would endeavor to ride in between the herd and their accustomed watering place and keep them moving slowly anywhere on the prairie away from water. It was useless to try to run them down, as a wild riderless horse could easily keep out of reach of a horse carrying a rider. So we first learned where all the watering places were and kept our quarry away from all water, while we grazed and watered our own mounts as often as desired. We then forced our wild band to travel as far as possible while we covered as little country as possible in our continuous chase. To keep them from getting to a watering place during the night, we would keep them up in a blind canyon or some strategic place where we could close them in and hold them as quietly as possible until daylight. Then we would again keep them on the move and away from water. We always worked in relays to save our own horses, and if we were successful in keeping our wild horses on dry grass and moving for four or five days we could ride them down, one at a time, and get close enough to rope them with our lariats.

Another way often used by the Sioux was to pick out a blind canyon with no easy way out and then drive a bunch of wild horses into this natural corral and rope them one at a time.

Either of these methods is somewhat hazardous for the captors, as I have seen wild horses, and especially the stallions, literally run over horse and rider in their attempt to escape. I know of no fiercer fighter on the range than a wild, striking, and biting stallion.

The most frightening moment of my life which also came very near being my last, was looking up into the wide-open jaws and bared teeth of a big, black, wild stallion which had broken from his cornered band. He made a mad rush at the horse I was riding and struck him on the side of the head with his front hoofs, at the same time tearing a great hole in my horse's shoulder with his teeth. We were piled up in a heap, after which the big stallion leaped clear of us and escaped down the canyon. My horse was hit and bitten so badly that he had to be destroyed immediately.

Another method of capturing wild horses, occasionally used by Indians and cowboys alike, is that of creasing, or temporarily stunning them by a well-placed steel-jacket rifle bullet in the fleshy part of the neck between the top of the neck and the spinal cord. This stuns them for a few minutes, in which time the hunter can ride up and tie down his horse. This takes some pretty accurate shooting at long distances, as it is difficult to get very close to a bunch of wild horses on the open prairie.

While out on the prairie, it often was necessary to picket or secure our horses for one reason or another. Wild horses will fight hard to escape, but the Indian learned how to tie his ponies securely, where there is no snubbing post, tree, rock, or even a bush to tie to. He simply tied them to a hole in the ground. If a prairie dog or gopher hole can be found, well and good; he pushes a couple feet of his rope down the hole and with his hunting knife, he digs a small hole large enough to put his arm in, cutting the hole at an angle to meet the hole where his rope is a couple feet down. When the new hole meets the end of the rope he pulls it up through with his hand and ties it above the ground. This V-shaped hole in the ground, a couple feet deep, will hold an ox team. If no gopher hole is handy, he digs the complete V-shaped anchor himself.

A horse on a lariat thus securely tied to a hole in the ground will be within rope length of that anchor when you come looking for him again. You may well rest assured of that.

Many travelers in the Badlands and in the alkalied country of the West, and more especially the Southwest, have suffered because of water, not necessarily because of the lack of water entirely, but because of mineral or poisonous properties in some waterholes found on the desert. Sometimes the clearest water is bad and muddy water may be good to drink. The Indian and cowboy long ago learned that certain desert springs are so saturated with alkalies, arsenic, or other mineral deposits that the water can be quite disagreeable or even harmful. But the Indian has only to pick up a handful of common soil and throw it in the suspected spring or waterhole. If the water remains muddy looking, from the handful of soil, the water is safe to drink, but should it all settle and clear immediately or turn yellowish, the alkali or chemical is strong enough to cause harm.

Next to the horse, the eagle is perhaps the most cherished possession of an Indian brave. The feathers of this bird are in the mink-coat class of personal adornment. There is no more prized or beautiful part of an Indian's costume than his eagle-feather war bonnet or headdress. This headdress is made from the long tail feathers only, and as one eagle possesses but twelve tail feathers, it requires from three to four eagles to make one bonnet.

Eagles are not common, even in the Western Indian country, and their habit of soaring to great heights and of building nests in remote high mountain crags and in the tallest trees, makes their capture no easy matter. When I was a small lad, Big Elk taught me how to shoot eagles in flight. We used a strong hickory bow, which usually was about as long as we were tall. The steel-pointed arrows were about half as long as was the bow. These bows required considerable strength for the customary standing shot or shooting from the backs of ponies, but for hunting eagles in flight we would lie on our backs on the ground and hold the bow with our moccasined feet and pull back the string with both hands. By so doing our aim was fairly accurate and we could send an arrow completely out of sight. However, even eagles look very small at so great a height. I have shot hundreds of arrows at high-soaring eagles, but was successful only once in bringing down the bird.

The most successful way of capturing eagles is with the Indian eagle trap, arranged near where they are fairly plentiful. This is made by digging a hole in the ground five to six feet deep and about the same size in diameter. This is covered over with slender poles and brush, after which a live grouse or sage hen or the carcass of some small animal is placed on the top. In all cases, the bait is securely tied so that it cannot be carried away readily. One or more persons conceal themselves in this pit, with blankets and food for a prolonged stay. Quietly they wait and watch for some soaring or nearby eagle. When the great bird begins soaring in a circle overhead, slowly descending, the hidden hunters watch breathlessly for the eagle to light on or near their bait. When finally he does light on the brush over the trap, one of the hunters carefully, but quickly, reaches up through the brush covering, grabs the eagle by one or both legs, and suddenly jerks the unsuspecting bird down into the pit. The other hunter throws a blanket over and around the powerful captive and smothers or strangles it as soon as possible, as the powerful claws or beak can spell sudden disaster to its captors.

Young Walking Buffalo Bull and I were not more than twelve or thirteen years old when we decided to do ourselves the honor of capturing an eagle in our own trap, singlehanded. We had heard the older Indians tell about capturing eagles for their war bonnets, and had seen several traps being prepared, so we knew the secret.

We arose very early and brought a blanket and some food for our all-day watch in the pit; we also shot a jack rabbit to use as bait. We tied it securely on the brush cover and waited for our prospective captive. Along in the middle of the forenoon, Walking Buffalo Bull saw an eagle soaring high over our heads. We watched breathlessly and after some time he circled and landed near our trap. After a long pause, he finally hopped over and began tearing at our anchored rabbit. Walking Bull was to reach up and grab his legs and I was to throw the blanket over the eagle and jump on it and break its back.

When the proper moment arrived, Walking Bull quickly grabbed the eagle's legs and pulled him down through the cover, bringing most of the slender sticks and brush down on top of us with the eagle. Somehow, Bull slipped or stumbled on the floor of our trap, and instead of throwing the blanket over the fiercely flopping captive, I wrapped it around my own neck and we wound up with all three of us under the blanket in a heap in one corner. Our faces and eyes were full of falling dirt, and we found we had trapped one eagle we wished we didn't have. That thirty pounds of bird claws and feathers put up a fight such as I never want to see again. We were two pretty badly mussed-up and frightened eagle hunters before that Prince of the Clouds found his way out of the den and we were really most happy to be rid of our fighting captive. The eagle clawed Bull up pretty badly and to this day he still carries many deep scars across his back and shoulders to remind him of our first eagle trap.

One of the favorite pastimes of the plains Indians is dancing. These dances have a three-fold purpose — amusement, worship, and an appeal for superhuman help. Among the many ceremonial dances of the Sioux is the Sun Dance, called by the Dakotas "An-pa-wi Wa-che-pi." I have attended many of these tribal dances, given by my adopted people, and took part in several when I was a young man. The Sun Dance is, perhaps, one of the least known and least understood by the white man. The Dakota nation and the Kan-gi-wi-ca-sa, or Crow Tribe, of Montana, still hold the Sun Dance ceremony, each midsummer, on their reservations. These are attended by all members of their respective tribes and, occasionally, by ranchers and white people of the neighboring vicinity. The last ceremonial Sun Dance, to which I was the invited guest of Chief Max Big Man, was held on Pryor Creek, in southern Montana, late in August, 1947.

The encampment was composed of some three hundred lodges, arranged in a circle of about half a mile in diameter, on a flat mesa near the creek. In the center of this circle was marked out a place for erecting the pavilion. About noon of the first day, several hundred mounted men rode back and forth over the ground where the pavilion was to be set up, for about an hour, yelling and singing to scare the evil spirits away, as was the custom of their ancestors. After this, a number of the older men rode down to the creek and, with considerable ceremony, chopped down a cottonwood tree to be used as the sacred pole. When the tree went down a charge was made on it by several men, after which the tree, branches and all, was taken up and carried by the men to the Sun Dance grounds, a distance of about a mile. The branches were then all stripped off and the pole set up in the ground. Around this pole they erected the dance pavilion in a circle of about sixty feet in diameter. The pavilion was constructed by setting posts in the ground around the extreme outer edge about ten feet high. Using the center pole for a brace, small poles were laid on top, slanting slightly toward the outer edge. This pole frame was then covered with boughs. The sacred pole was decorated with red, white, and blue colored banners, gifts to the Great Spirit.

Some two or three hundred dancers marched around the enclosure, dancing, singing, and drawing bows, pretending to be shooting up at the pole. That evening, at sundown, the Sun Dancers proper, thirty-six in number, entered the enclosure, followed by the medicine man, who painted four rings around the sacred pole with red paint, to signify that the Sun Dance ceremony was to last four days and nights. The thirty-six Sun Dancers would not be allowed to partake of any food or water during the ceremonial dance. Each of these dancers was given a whistle, made of the wing bone of an eagle, with a small white feather tied on the end. They stood in a circle next to the outer edge of the enclosure facing the sacred pole. Near the entrance was placed a large drum, surrounded by six or eight old men, who beat the tom tom and chanted for the dancers. They danced to the rhythmic beat of the drummers and blew the small whistles in time to their steps, all the time gazing steadily at the sun. During the sunless hours, they kept their eyes steadily on a buffalo skull and a stuffed eagle suspended at the top of the sacred pole. The Sun Dancers were barefooted and wore blankets belted around their waists, their upper bodies being bare except for beaded necklaces and arm bands and narrow bead bandeaus around their heads. Several dancers wearing their hair in long braids decorated the braids with beads or colored yarn. The drummers changed at any time they desired, but the Sun Dancers kept up their dance for four days and four nights without food or water. They slowly dance up to the sacred pole and then back again to the edge of the circle in the same path but always facing the sacred pole in the center.

Occasionally a dancer would pass out from exhaustion, especially after the third or fourth day. When they fell in the pavilion no one was allowed to assist them in any way or even come near them. Sometimes some of the dancers had to dance around the fallen one, but only the ceremonial medicine man was allowed to come near him. He danced around the unconscious dancer, chanting and covering him with an eagle wing fan. I have seen Sun Dancers remain unconscious for several hours and on two occasions participants have died from over-exertion.

In the early days, both the Crows and the Sioux finished the dance by tying a willing dancer to the sacred pole. A rawhide thong was fastened to the breast or back of the dancer by running the thong under the skin. This operation was performed by raising the skin of the breast or back, and cutting two slits about an inch long through the uplifted skin. Then a wooden skewer was inserted through the slits, fastened by sinews, and the sinews were tied to a rope or thong. The rope was tied to the upper end of the pole, and the dancer ran forward or backward from the pole endeavoring to break loose. This displayed the bravery and courage of the dancer. I have seen many of the older Indians with Sun Dance scars on their breasts and backs. These self-torture dances are seldom seen nowadays, but the Sun Dance is still very popular among many of the plains tribes.

Another dance that still remains a mystery to the paleface, and the medical world, is the age-old Snake Dance ceremony of the Hopi Indians, of Arizona. Some people who have witnessed this dance believe that the rattlesnakes used in the ceremony have had the poison removed before being handled by the dancers. This is an error. None of these snakes has ever been relieved of its natural poison, or drugged in any way. Prior to the time of the dance, the Hopis go out on the desert and procure dozens of rattlesnakes by means of a forked stick which they place over the snake's body just back of the head. This holds the snake fast and safe while the captor catches the snake with his hand just back of the jaws and places him in a box or rawhide container. In this way the snakes are brought in to the pueblo and placed in the snake pit for the coming ceremony.

Meanwhile the persons who are to participate in the snake dance go into a kiva or sweat lodge where they remain for about twenty days. These lodges are prepared by heating many stones on an outside fire after which they are placed on sticks and brought into the sweat lodge, where water is sprinkled over them by the medicine man. This produces a steam bath for the naked men inside. These men, who are to be the snake dancers in the ceremony, are also regularly given a brew of a sacred drink, along with light food. It is this sacred brew that keeps them from harm when bitten by the poisonous snakes, and is the real secret of this mysterious dance. The brew, which resembles a very black coffee or dark heavy medicine, contains the properties which act as an antitoxin against the poison of the rattler. I have seen this brew several times, also the many ingredients that are combined to make it, but I was never told what it was composed of. It contains certain barks, leaves, berries, roots, and other natural medicated items, but what they are or the proportions used is known only to the tribal medicine man and his protégé. Even the other members of the tribe claim not to know the secrets.

When the dancer has gone through the proper period of sweat bath and consumed enough of the mysterious brew, he is ready for the ceremonial Snake Dance. He then enters the snake pit with the other dancers and dozens of very lively desert rattlesnakes. They are not in the slightest danger from the many snakes, and I assure you the snakes are fully equipped with all their savagery and natural poison. I have watched these Hopi dancers go through their ceremonial dances, holding a wildly striking rattler in each hand and one between his teeth, and have sat in awe while two of these snakes struck the dancer on the breast and full in the face, with no harmful results. These same dancers told me that their immunity wears off in a few days after the completion of these herb sweat baths. They say also that if any normal, healthy person, white or Indian, should go through this same herb and sweat bath process, their bodies would be made immune in a like manner. After the ceremonial Snake Dance is over, all the snakes are taken back to the desert again and released, as it is bad medicine for any Hopi to kill a snake.

The Dakotas have no family or surnames, but the children of a family have particular pet names which belong to them in the order of their birth, up to and including the fifth child. The names are: Chaske, Hepan, Hepi, Chatan, and Hake. For the girls they are: Winona, Hapan, Hapistinna, Wanske, and Wihake. Thus the first child, if a boy, is called, Chaske, if a girl, Winona. The second, if a boy, is called Hepan, and if a girl, Hapan, etc. If there are more than five children in the family, the others have no names of this kind. These childhood names usually are retained by the children only for a short time, and more often than not they are given an additional name at birth.

These names are selected in several ways and one young

warrior may have several names during his lifetime. His first name is received through some circumstance surrounding his birth. For instance, if, as the baby is being born, or soon after, a wolf should be heard to howl near the tepee, the baby would likely be called "Howling Wolf." Should the mother see an eagle soaring over her lodge soon after his birth, she might name him Swift Eagle, Flying Eagle, Soaring Eagle, or High Eagle, as the incident might appeal to her. Sometimes the child is given a name by his father or grandfather, or by some other member of the tribe. A great feast often accompanies the ceremony of the giving of such names. Often too, when they are older, they may receive the imposing and honorable names of some of their famous ancestors, such as Black Bear, Running Buffalo, Brave Bull, or Standing Bear. If he goes on the war-path and distinguishes himself among his tribesmen, he may receive the warlike name of Kills-the-Enemy, Plenty Coups, or Young-Man-Afraid-of-His-Horse, which, literally, means They (the foe) fear even his horse. A great warrior might have as many as eight or ten names during his lifetime.

The tribal council is, perhaps, the most important of all tribal gatherings. Here all the important laws and decisions of tribal interest are discussed and settled. The chief calls the council and selects those who shall participate, but these tribal affairs usually are composed of the oldest and most important members of the tribe. The council members are invited to the lodge of the chief, or, occasionally, to the spacious tepee of some prominent member of the tribe. The meetings are most solemn occasions. When all have arrived and arranged themselves in a circle on the ground, the chief gets ready the ceremonial red stone pipe and, lighting it, he offers it first to the east, then to the south, the west, and the north, to the Great Spirit and to Mother Earth and, after much deliberation, he rises and speaks. He may call on certain ones to speak or wait for anyone who volunteers his counsel. In any case, each one waits long and silently before beginning his answer or speech. The Indian is a natural orator and his reasoning is far more elaborate than might be supposed. Many a red man's eulogy would well be worthy of record. What more eloquent speech of few words could be made in any language than that of Chief Joseph, the great war chief of the Nez Perce. He surrendered to the far superior United States forces on a bleak winter's day in 1877, when he and his starving tribesmen were surrounded on the snow-covered plains of northern Montana. As he handed his war club to his captors these were his immortal words: "Our warriors are all dead. Our women and children are cold. We have no blankets. I am tired of fighting. And I am getting old. From where the sun now stands I will fight no more forever."

It was an old friend of mine, Chief Plenty Coups, of the Crow Nation, who was once asked, in my presence, what he thought of the treatment of his people by the white man. He thought long, but his answer was short. He said: "Nothing the white man has given us can make up for the happy, carefree life we knew when the vast prairies were still unfenced. Then we never worried; we had plenty to eat and plenty to keep us warm. Now the white man has killed all our buffalo; he has taken all our land. Now he wants to tell us how to live while starving us." The white man has often promised his red brothers some wonderful things in bold print, but when the fine print was finally interpreted, the Indian found himself holding the proverbial sack.

It was some years ago that I had the rare privilege of being invited to a very important Sioux council, which several high officials from Washington were to attend. It appears that some misunderstanding had occurred between the department represented by them and the tribesmen. During the discussion, an elderly gentleman from the department was standing in the center of half a hundred silent and attentive Dakotas. For the third time the visitor was loudly appealing to his listeners. "My red brothers," he continued, "sixty long years have whitened this old gray head of mine and I never have been known to cheat one of my red brothers." With this he closed his long speech and smilingly sat down.

A long silence ensued, and then a little old man arose from

his seat on the ground and, wrapping his red blanket more closely around him, quietly but abruptly spoke thus. "Paleface brother, I have listened long and thoughtfully to your big talk, and I respect your old gray head. But please look at me. Seventy long winters have blown over my old white head, but they haven't blown away my brains." And with that the council came to a close.

Some years ago, several tourists from a little New England village were fishing and sightseeing along the Yellowstone River, which is known to the Sioux as "Un-pan Wa-kpa" or Elk River. It so happened that the Cheyennes were having one of their annual ceremonial dances and feasts. The tourists were enjoying the dances and taking numerous pictures of each other with various groups of the gaily costumed dancers. As the day wore on, several of the Indian families began getting ready for their noonday meal. The boiled stew in the big kettle over the campfire looked inviting enough and our New Englanders thought it would be a novel idea to dine with one of the Indian families, and a picture of their group thus eating with the prairie people, would also be something to show the neighbors back home. So one of the gentlemen of the party made himself useful around one of the campfires, by carrying several armloads of wood and placing it on the fire under one of the large kettles, at the same time striking up a sort of pidgin-English conversation with the members of the family around the fire. This had the desired results of being asked to join them and partake of the coming meal. He and his group readily accepted with pleasure and much anticipation.

They soon sat around the steaming kettle amongst the Indian families and gladly handed their plates to the elderly woman who was dishing out the contents in large dippers full. The stew was delicious. Several of the tourists debated among themselves just what the meat might be: buffalo, beef, venison, or sage hen. The spokesman of the group however, was certain that the savory stew was duck, his favorite meat. And besides, he desired to show his extreme fondness and appreciation to his hosts, and to display a little of his worldly knowledge and Western experience and his learning in the language of the Indians. He again handed his plate to the elderly woman. "Heap good, very much heap good cook, please me have more quack-quack meat?" he asked with a broad friendly smile. The old Indian woman smiled aprovingly, and gladly refilled his plate, adding "Yes thanks, very much glad you like, heap good bow-wow."

The Dakota folklore is full of legends of their tribe, and of the origin of the various animals, birds, and inhabitants of the waters. (A legend of the great flood can be found in many Indian languages, as accurate as we read it in the Bible, and no doubt it predates the Bible itself by many centuries.)

One of the many interesting Dakota legends I heard around our lodge campfire as a youth, parallels one I heard in my school days about the Arab's tent and the camel. Once upon a time, long, long ago, there was a Badger named Hoka, who was very rich and had many children. He was possessed of a bow and one mysterious arrow. There was no other arrow like it in all the land, but he could shoot this mysterious arrow only once each day. In the bend of a river he had a buffalo corral to which buffalo came every morning, led by a phantom buffalo bull. From this corral, Badger made a very straight path down the river, for the buffalo to follow as they were driven from the corral. Each morning as they started out on the one straight path, he ran swiftly around the herd and concealed himself at the far end of the trail. Then when they were all in a straight line, he shot his mysterious arrow into the first buffalo, which passed through the whole herd. So Badger became very rich in dried buffalo meat.

Then one day there came Mato Hota, a Gray Bear, to his lodge. And Gray Bear said, "Wonderful, my brother, that you should live here in such abundance, while I and my children are starving. Could you give me some meat?"

The Badger said, "Yes, you are my brother, so I will give you some meat for you and your starving children." So when the Gray Bear was starting home, Badger gave him a bundle of dried buffalo meat to carry home.

The next morning, Gray Bear again came to the lodge of Badger and said, "The buffalo meat you gave me was very large and it tired me to carry it home. Can I bring my family and live in your lodge, that I do not have to carry the meat?" The Badger was a very kind-hearted person, so gave Gray Bear permission to bring his family to live with him. So the next morning, Gray Bear came with his household, and as soon as he moved in, Badger was turned out, and Gray Bear took possession of all his meat. The Badger then lived out-doors and starved.

The next morning after he took possession, Gray Bear awoke very early in the morning and, standing outside, said, "You Badger, come get up, your corral is full of Buffalo." So the Badger took his bow and mysterious arrow and, as he was accustomed to do, shot it through the whole line of buffalo. But the Gray Bear took them all and did not let the Badger have even one.

This he did, morning after morning, but never did he give the Badger one for his own use, and so Badger and his children were about to die of hunger. But every morning the youngest of Gray Bear's children was given a large buffalo shoulder to eat, and when he saw the Badger was dying of hunger he ate but little himself, giving Badger most of his meat. Thus Badger and his family maintained an existence.

Again, one morning very early, the Gray Bear ordered the Badger to take his bow and arrow and kill more buffalo, but he was so weak with hunger that he refused, and Gray Bear said, "I will crush you if you don't kill for me the buffalo." But Badger was so weak with hunger that he could not rise, so Gray Bear was about to crush him. Then Gray Bear's youngest son took many buffalo shoulders to Badger's cave and hid them for Badger to eat. However, when Gray Bear found out his son was giving Badger meat he was very angry and ran after his son to crush him, but as he was running away, Badger saw him in danger and hid him in his cave with his own children.

The next night, Gray Bear's son returned to his father's

lodge and took all the meat and brought it to his friend Badger. Then the family of Gray Bear had to leave the lodge of Badger and move far away, and soon Badger and his family and Gray Bear's son were all happy again. And that is why the Gray Bear has to sleep all winter so that Badger can hunt for food as much as he likes.

Another legend often related to me by Cloud Woman was the Dakota story of Ptan Sapa, or the Black Otter. In the days of long, long ago there were six children of a very poor otter family — five brothers and one sister. All the brothers were of different color — one was red, one was blue, one yellow, one white, and one black — and the little sister also was black. Their parents were very, very old and very poor. So the five brothers had to work very hard to take care of their parents, and the sister stayed always home to keep the lodge fire burning. The four sons who had the beautiful red, blue, yellow, and white fur skins were very proud and never liked to get their beautiful furs wet or dirty, so they did nothing all day long but look at themselves in the clear water, while their brother, the black otter, hunted and gathered food for the lazy brothers and the very old and poor parents.

Every day they would eat all that the black otter could fetch home so that the old parents, the sister, and the black otter were always very hungry. After a time the old people became so starved that they died. The sister and the black otter carried them away and buried them in a mound by a beautiful stream, but the brothers with the pretty furs would not even help them dig the graves. Then the otters with the beautiful furs moved into the lodge of their aged parents and forced the black otter and the sister to live outdoors.

When the black otter came near their lodge, his four brothers would take his food and chase him away, saying that they did not want other animal people to know that they were of the same family. This made the black otter and his sister very angry, so they waited until all four of the other otters went down to the stream to look at their beautiful furs in the clear water. Then they hid themselves in the lodge and, as the brothers came in one by one, the black otter and his sister beat them over the head with their war clubs until they were unconscious and then threw them into the fire where they became black all over. That is why, they say, that now there are only black otters.

Big Elk told me this story many times, as handed down by his people centuries ago. Once upon a time, many, many years ago, there were many peoples who lived in a far-away land. They were very wicked and they fought much among themselves and with all the people who were near them. This made the Great Spirit very angry, as he wanted his people to live in peace with each other. However, some listened to his voice and some did not. When he found that the people did not obey him, he created a great turtle and commanded all the good people to come and get on the turtle's back, as he would destroy all the people who did not. Many people believed the Great Spirit and got on the turtle's back, but most of the bad people did not believe the thunder voice and would not do as he commanded.

Then the great turtle walked down to the water, which rose and covered all the land. Then the turtle swam for many, many suns and, finally, came to a place where he found a small piece of land showing out of the water. The land rose higher and higher and became larger and larger and the thunder voice of the Great Spirit commanded these people to leave the back of the great turtle and live on the land forever after. This, the Dakota legend says, is how the Indian people came to live here.

Many are the suns and moons and winters that have passed since that time. So ends my story.

Chapter XVIII

The Hermit of Hidden Canyon

SANDY MC LARAN WAS BORN ON A LITTLE FARM IN MONROE County, Pennsylvania, just across the river from the Delaware Water Gap. When the Civil War broke out, Sandy was a young man of eighteen. He enlisted in the Pennsylvania volunteers.

About this time another young man, also eighteen, enlisted in the service; his name was Jacob Wagner. However, Jacob was not from a small farm, neither was he from the Delaware. He was born on a plantation along the Cumberland Mountains, in Tennessee. The uniform he wore was not blue; it was gray.

The close friendship of Jacob and Sandy began under strange and unusual circumstances. They did not meet on any field of battle. Jacob and Sandy met in famed Libby Prison. Not many months after Sandy left his little farm home along the Delaware he was taken prisoner, and remained a captive until peace was declared. The prisoners were not treated well in these camps. Food and clothing were scarce even for the best equipped of the troops, and prison fare was even worse.

Jacob, although a young man, had received a good education and training for his time, and had been appointed a clerk and food dispenser at the prison. Sandy was a jolly and likeable young fellow and Jacob assigned him to assist in several of his duties. They soon took a liking to each other and Jacob saw to it that Sandy often received an extra supply of food. Both boys had read and heard much of the opportunities of the West and each expressed a desire to go out into the new gold country of Montana, as soon as the war ended. When the war did end, each of the boys returned to his home. However, Sandy never forgot the boy in gray who treated him with so much kindness during his long months in Libby Prison. After a while Sandy wrote to his Southern friend and arranged to meet him in St. Louis in the spring of 1866. From here the two boys took passage on the Missouri River steamer, "Far West."

One sunny day in May they steamed into the frontier town of Fort Benton, Montana, the nearest navigable point to the new gold fields. From here they took a stage to Bannack, where rich strikes were being worked. Bannack, the first capital of Montana territory, was already a thriving, bustling camp of several thousand prospectors and miners. Thousands of dollars were being taken out of rich gravel claims every day. All the good claims had been taken by the time Sandy and Jacob arrived, and many miners had already moved on over the Ruby Range to where a prospector named Fairweather had made a rich strike on Alder Gulch, some two hundred miles east. This new camp had acquired the name of Virginia City, and the original capital at Bannack had been moved to the new camp on Alder Creek.

Virginia City was a typical frontier mining town. Claims were staked for miles up and down the gulch. Saloons and hurdy-gurdy houses were wide open twenty-four hours a day. Gold dust filled every miner's poke and was the medium of exchange in all mining camps in the West. The grass had not yet grown over the graves of Club Foot George Ives and his notorious band of road agents, and Bummer Dan was still washing a hundred dollars a pan from his claim on the west side of the gulch.

Sandy and Jacob found a claim a couple of miles north of the Virginia City camp and began their first venture in mining gold. Their take averaged some five or six dollars to the pan. Nothing compared to some of the claims farther up the gulch, but the two young soldiers were very well satisfied. They worked on their claims until 1874. They never gambled their gold and during the eight years had accumulated a fair amount of money. As their claims had been pretty well worked out, Sandy and Jacob decided to move farther north and go into the stock-raising business together. Texas cattle were now being brought north to Montana in large drives, and the Montana buffalo grass was found to be an excellent all-year-around feed.

They stayed around Fort Benton, western boat terminal on the Missouri River, for a while and did some freighting over the Mullan road from Fort Benton to the new mines in Idaho. They were engaged in the overland freight business but, not liking the monotony of the slow-moving freight teams, they went up to the Milk River country, on the Canadian Border. There they took up a ranch and began raising cattle and horses. Their new venture proved successful and they found a ready market for all the cattle and horses they wished to dispose of. Freighters needed good horses, and mining camps were willing buyers of fat beeves.

In 1878, while on a freight trip to a Canadian trading post, Jacob was attacked by a party of highwaymen and killed. However, he sold his life dearly, as two of the four masked road agents also were killed in the fierce gun fight. Sandy, grieved over the loss of his boyhood army friend and loyal partner of fourteen years, wrote to the family in the Tennessee mountains and related the story of Jacob's death. Later he sent them the money which was Jacob's share of the partnership.

Sandy continued on his ranch alone for a couple of years and one day when a party of Blackfeet Indians was camped near his ranch on the Milk River, Sandy saw an unusually pretty young maiden of the tribe, and soon she became the center of his attentions. This interesting maiden was the daughter of a Blackfeet chief, and her name was Morning

Star. Many a young brave of the band had looked upon this slender, dark-eyed maiden with lovelorn eyes, but the wily old chief, knowing of the charms and value of his beautiful daughter, had scorned all offers for her hand. Sandy was smitten at first sight, and the next day he procured several gaily colored Hudson Bay blankets and four of his best saddle ponies and offered them at the chief's tepee door for the object of his heart. After some time and consideration the chief gave his consent, and it appears that the dark-eyed maiden was a very willing party in the transaction. She also had liked the handsome rancher and was happy to go with him to his humble log cabin down the river.

Sandy had been in the Blackfeet country since taking up the ranch on Milk River, so could speak his bride's native language with little difficulty. They were very happy together. He gave her many ponies of her own and she proved to be an excellent rider. Soon she could care for the stock as well as Sandy himself. They worked hard and prospered, supplying horses to many freight outfits and meat to the many mining camps in the mountains to the west of them. A couple of years after Morning Star had come to the home of her sandy-haired lover, she presented him with a bright-eyed, dark-haired baby daughter.

The Blackfeet occasionally camped near Sandy's ranch, and often Morning Star would go and stay several days with her people. Although she never said much about her trips, Sandy could see she still had a longing for the carefree camp life of her people.

In 1882, Sandy received word from his old home in Pennsylvania that his parents had died and had left the family homestead to him and a younger sister, whom he had not seen since he left home in 1866. He longed to return to the place of his childhood and see his sister and the old home he left eighteen years before, but his chief concern was for Morning Star and the baby. She had been loyal and a faithful and helpful companion. To take her with him on a trip to the East would be a difficult undertaking, and she would never be contented or happy among a people so strange and different. She did not wish to leave her people and he was very unhappy at the thought of leaving her and their baby alone so long, as a trip to the East would take many months. The winter was coming on and the last river boat from Fort Benton would not return until the following spring.

Some of the Blackfeet along the border had also made several raids on neighboring ranches and settlements because of some misunderstanding between the settlers on boundary lines. Also Louis Riel and his half-breed renegade followers were stirring up an Indian rebellion along the border. A few of the white settlers of the Milk River country had doubted Morning Star's loyalty to her husband and white friends, in case of trouble with the Blackfeet. And her frequent visits among the Blackfeet were naturally looked upon with suspicion by some of her own people. She and Sandy alike were torn between their love for each other and the blood ties of their own people.

With a great deal of reluctance and a much saddened heart Sandy started out for Fort Benton, some three hundred miles away. He took his best saddle horse and a pack outfit. The horses he could leave at a friend's ranch near Benton, picking them up again on his return the following spring. He would pass through Blackfeet country and he would have to be cautious. Sandy traveled until dusk on the first day and camped in a little cottonwood grove. The second day brought him into the Blackfeet buffalo-hunting country, so he was a little more watchful of his course; however, the day was uneventful. Late in the afternoon, he located a good place to camp in a willow-covered creek bottom. Here he built a fire and cooked his supper among the trees, after which he took his horses and bedroll across the creek and made his camp in a small coulee about half a mile above the grove of willows. He arranged his bed in a location overlooking his campfire, but quite out of sight of anyone traveling along the creek. With his horses picketed in another coulee just over a low hill, Sandy felt he was well protected from anyone who might be in the vicinity and find his recently made campfire. He made up his bedroll and lay down for the night, his six-shooter under his buckskin coat pillow and his Winchester alongside him in the bed. About midnight, he got up to change the picket rope on his horses and see that they were feeding quietly, and noticed that both horses seemed unusually alert and uneasy. They would graze for a brief time and then quickly turn their ears forward and look intently in the direction of the creek. Sandy understood the habits of range animals and knew that their actions were not to go unheeded. He had only his Colt tucked in his belt around his waist and, speaking a reassuring word to his horses, he cautiously walked back to his bed. The moon was shining brightly, and he could see for a considerable distance. Taking his Winchester, he walked back and saddled up one of his horses, leaving him still picketed on the long rope.

Indians ordinarily do not travel at night, but Sandy was taking no chances of being taken by surprise. His horses still were uneasy, so he crept up on the hill between, and overlooking, the horses and his bed. This also gave him a view of the camp where he had built his fire in the willows. He lay quietly on the brow of the hill and scanned the country all around him. Soon the eastern sky began to gray and he could see farther into the distant hills and ravines. Some distance down the valley he thought he could faintly make out a moving object. It was moving in his direction, and soon he could see someone leading a horse up the same trail he had come over the evening before. He knew by the way the person was stopping occasionally and bending down close to the trail that it was an Indian following a trail. This would indicate that Indians were camped somewhere in the vicinity and, knowing of the hostile attitude of some of the Blackfeet, Sandy knew that such a party could mean trouble. Also, if this lone scout believed that anyone was still in the vicinity he would give word to his party, who would search the entire country to locate him, and Sandy's chances of escape would be difficult, if not impossible.

The lone Indian and his led horse were coming closer to

where he was watching. The gray streak in the East was beginning to give Sandy a clearer outline of the approaching Indian. He could now see clearly enough to draw sight along his Winchester and could now be fairly sure of hitting the Indian before he himself would be seen. He maneuvered slowly into position for a long shot and took careful aim. To miss would mean that the scout would escape with the information that Sandy was still in the vicinity. He steadied himself holding his breath for an instant before pressing the trigger. Just the second before the shot would have echoed down the valley, Sandy's horse whinnied, answered by a familiar sound down the valley. Then a voice called out, "Sandy, Sandy." Sandy lowered his rifle. He could not believe his ears; the voice was that of his wife, Morning Star. He stood up and waved his arms in the semi-darkness, and then ran down the hill to meet her. She told him her story.

Soon after Sandy started out, Morning Star had received word from some of her people that several of the young braves had left the village and had gone south across the Marias, and she was afraid they might run into Sandy before he reached Fort Benton. She went on further to explain how she had left their home immediately, and followed the trail of his two horses. She had started out with four horses, riding one and driving the rest, always changing her mount for a fresh one and leaving the ridden horse on the trail to be picked up on her return home. At this time she had been riding and leading her remaining horse, depending on the clearness of the trail she was following. She knew that Sandy would travel slowly on his long journey, and figured to overtake him in two or three days. She had seen his old campfire site and knew about when she could expect to overtake him.

She accompanied Sandy on to Fort Benton and brought his horses back to Milk River, where they would be reunited when the first river boat came up from St. Louis in the spring.

As the winter months waned into the warm days of spring, the melting snows and breaking ice again foretold it was time for the familiar old rear-wheeler river boats to start their slow navigation once more up the winding Missouri. Morning Star was waiting when the first boat slowly pointed its bow alongside the old wooden wharf at Benton. As usual, the old flat-bottomed boat was piled high with miners' equipment and merchandise for the ranchers and supply posts of the upper river country. Sandy was among the hundred or so passengers who had made the long slow journey from the States. Morning Star's baby had died during the long winter and many of their horses had been driven off and stolen by the Blackfeet and roving bands of Crees along the border.

Due to the approaching rebellion of Louis Riel and his Cree followers in the vicinity, Sandy decided to leave the Milk River country and locate farther south along the Missouri River in Montana territory. He had liked the picturesque country along the Missouri between the Judith and the Musselshell Rivers. Here could be found good hunting, trapping, some mining, and abundant feed and natural shelter for his stock.

They crossed the Bear Paw Mountains and followed Cow Creek to where it emptied into the Missouri. There they followed the north bank down the river in the direction of the Musselshell to where the high rock bluffs begin on the south side of the Missouri channel. Here, Sandy found a long, narrow canyon leading south from the river and widening into a small grassy valley some distance from the river. The little valley gave him ample, well-protected room for his log cabin and corrals. From the river it would scarcely be noticed as a canyon leading back into the rugged hills. He called it the Hidden Canyon.

They built their low, two-room log-cabin ranch house and corrals that first summer and were secure for the coming winter. Their stock, unfamiliar with the newly located range, had to be watched closely until such time as they would cease drifting away. Sandy hunted and trapped during the winter and their food supply was always plentiful. Morning Star was well learned in the ways of her people, so that Sandy always had plenty of beautifully beaded leggings and jackets to wear on his traplines.

One early spring morning Sandy missed a small band of his best horses. Upon further search over their accustomed range, he discovered where they had been driven across the river and headed north, probably by wandering Crees or horse rustlers. Sandy was busy with some other work on the ranch, so Morning Star went in search of the missing horses. She rode her favorite Indian pony and followed the tracks of the missing band. The day wore on and the sun was setting in the west. Sandy was wondering why Morning Star had not returned. From a high point back of his cabin he could see across the river and for miles in every direction. As the sun disappeared, Sandy climbed up to this promontory to see if he could see anything of the Indian girl and his horses. Gaining a high point he saw her in the distance driving the horses before her.

As it was now getting late, Sandy signalled her to leave the horses on their accustomed range and cross the river before it became too dark. The spring rains were not yet over and the Missouri was still above flood stage and very swift in many places. Sandy, anticipating where she would approach the opposite bank, went down to the stream and awaited the arrival of his courageous wife. The south bank of the river at this point is high allowing him to overlook the whole scene. The north side being low ground, was covered entirely with water for nearly half a mile.

Morning Star left her band of horses on the foothills as instructed and, having great faith in her pony, who had carried her through many a turbulent mountain stream, rode into the water on the flat. The faithful little horse breasted the surging water with all his usual vigor, plunging into the sink holes to scramble out again on the opposite side with his fearless rider clinging to his mane and shouting encouragement. Sandy watched the whole proceeding from the high bank on the opposite shore, with straining nerves and beating heart, powerless to render any assistance. Yet he had perfect confidence in the endurance of the little pony and the skill of his daring rider. But when they reached the current of the main stream, which rolled and surged like a mighty cataract he saw the little horse rise far out of the water, plunge forward, and disappear, to arise many many yards down the stream, but now riderless. Relieved of his burden, he swam straight for shore and scrambled up the steep bank and shook his wet hide.

Sandy's agony knew no bounds. He ran here and there, straining his eyes in vain for a glimpse of Morning Star. All night long he walked along the bank of the stream, but no call reached his ears. The sun rose bright and clear. The rains having ceased, the water began to recede. For several days, Sandy searched the banks and willows in vain. Finally, far below on the opposite side, among a raft of driftwood, he found the object of his search. He carefully carried her to a rocky point which extended out almost to the water's edge. High up on the side of this ledge, Sandy dug a cavity some distance into the loose rock and placed the remains of Morning Star, closing the opening with tightly wedged rocks.

Taking his horses and other belongings, he disappeared for several years from all human contact. In the spring of 1908, a couple of cowboys were riding in the vicinity and happened to notice a niche in the stone wall up on the bank and began taking out the loose rocks. When they had dug back a few feet they discovered a human skeleton, which they believed to be that of an Indian woman. They replaced the bones in the rock and threw back most of the stones. They mentioned it to several of their acquaintances and finally the incident came to the attention of several local papers as a news item.

One day, not long after, an old man with long, snowy-white hair appeared in the vicinity and looked over the location of the buried bones; he then took out the bones again, wrapped them in a blanket and departed. Soon stories began to circulate of an old, white-haired hermit living in an old deserted cabin up in Hidden Canyon. Several persons in the vicinity reported seeing the old man. He was always non-communicative and evaded them whenever possible. He had been seen once or twice in Malta, Zortman, and Lewistown with mink skins, martin, and muskrat, which he exchanged for provisions.

I had heard of the old man on numerous occasions, but never saw him but once. It was in 1911 when Lone Eagle and I were riding in the Missouri River brakes, and while camping along the river we saw an old man down by the river scaling some fish. His description corresponded with the stories we had heard of the Hermit of Hidden Canyon, so we tried to strike up a conversation with him, but without much success. Finally my brother addressed him in the Indian language accompanied by the corresponding Indian sign language. The old hermit looked with interest at my brother, and said, "You Injun?" My brother explained how he acquired his knowledge of the Indian dialect, and the old man became interested. My brother had met a few old members of the tribe to which his wife had belonged, and upon mentioning them, the old fellow began to talk of his younger days in the north Blackfeet country. We invited him to eat with us and were much surprised and pleased when he agreed to do so. During our conversation he told us of his old home along the Delaware, his experiences during the Civil War, and his trip to the Montana gold camps, and among the Blackfeet. He seemed glad to talk to someone of his life and experiences. We talked with him until late that night. His story was like a fantastic fairy tale, but we found it was all too true. His had been the venturous and romantic experiences of but few pioneer white men in our early West. He was truly the Hermit of Hidden Canyon. As the moon sank low in the western hills and the night became chilly, our venerable hermit bid us adieu and slowly walked up the trail to his humble log cabin.

We never saw him again. Two years later, in the early spring of 1913, my brother and I again had occasion to be in the Missouri River brakes country near Hidden Canyon, and, wondering how the old hermit had weathered the past severe winter, decided to pay him a visit. We finally found the narrow mouth of the canyon and slowly made our way up its rough, narrow trail. The brush was grown thick over the path and it didn't look as though anyone had traveled it for a long time. There had been a heavy snowfall during the winter and snow still covered the shaded portion of the canyon trail. We finally came to the old log cabin, but there were no tracks or signs of life anywhere visible. We pushed open the squeaky door and carefully walked in. There, lying on a low wooden bunk, made of deerskins and heavy sougans, were the remains of the old hermit. A few crude cooking utensils were near a rude fireplace. Farther back in the two-room cabin hung strips of jerked venison and dried fish. On a shelf in the back room was a crude chest made from roughly hewn cedar slabs, with a lid fastened on with elkskin hinges. In the chest were a pair of elkskin moccasins ornamented with porcupine quills, a few strings of beads, a lock of long black hair, and the bones of a human skeleton. On the inside of the lid was carved in rough letters, the name, Morning Star.

FLOYD SHUSTER MAINE (THE AUTHOR), BROTHER OF LONE EAGLE

Chapter XIX

Trip through the Enchanted Badlands

ACROSS THE HEART OF NORTH CENTRAL MONTANA STRETCHES A lonely scenic land, little changed since Lewis and Clark traversed it nearly a century and a half ago. This is perhaps the wildest, least-known, and least-accessible portion of the United States east of the Continental Divide. Here the Missouri River winds its way through glacial gorges and canyons of fantastic form, and from Fort Benton to Fort Peck, a distance of over two hundred miles, there is not one bridge, nor a single town. Few people realize that this mighty river, which has its source in southwestern Montana, is the longest river in North America, exceeding the Mississippi by over four hundred miles.

Since the only way to cross this mighty river is by fording or by a few small, fair-weather ferries, few Montanans and fewer outsiders have ever laid eyes on some of this most primitive and marvelous scenery in the United States. Up until the early '80's the Missouri River was the principal route of travel from St. Louis to the great gold fields and cattle country of the Northwest. Hundreds of fur traders, trappers, buffalo hunters, and gold seekers came up the river on the "Far West" and other famous boats. However, these early pioneers were merely passing through, on their way to Fort Benton, and but a small handful ever set foot on these wild, awe-inspiring badlands of the Missouri. There were only a few temporary trading posts and forts. Trappers, buffalo hunters, and prospectors occasionally camped within the area and a few wood cutters had established themselves along the river to supply the steam packets with fuel. Large bands of Indians also made their camps here while on their annual buffalo hunts. To be found in this vicinity are many high cliffs where the Indians drove great herds of buffalo over hundred-foot precipices.

NATURE AT HER BEST BORDERS THE QUEEN OF RIVERS

In more recent years, only a few hunters and cattle and sheep men, rounding up their animals, have seen this vast unsurveyed and unknown expanse of mystic wonderland. In fact, there are fewer inhabitants along this stretch of river today than there were in the early steamboat days. Lewis and Clark recorded this area as the most awe-inspiring and scenic part of America they had ever seen. I had often heard, from old Indian buffalo hunters, about the wonders and natural beauty of this part of the country, but it was not until the fall of 1913 that Lone Eagle and I saw this scenic wonderland. We left the Eagle Bar Ranch with our saddle ponies and a pack horse, and hit the Musselshell River at the mouth of Cat Creek. While riding down Cat Creek we noticed an unfinished sod house being built by a homesteader. Wondering just how a sod house was constructed, we turned off our course to look it over.

Several hundred wild longhorn cattle, recently brought into the basin from Texas and Old Mexico, were in the vicinity. These wild cattle would feed in our valley and get mixed up with our own more domesticated herds of white-faced short-horns and Herefords. We found out the quickest way to separate these longhorns from our own cattle was to ride into the entire mixed herd at a gallop, let out a couple good old Comanche yells and empty our six-guns over the heads of the herd. In less time than it takes to tell it, those longhorns would throw their heads and tails into the air and light out across the flats, leaving the slower-footed shorthorns far in the rear. All we had to do was to cut in between the two herds and turn back our own animals, while the longhorns soon faded out in the dust ahead.

A small herd of our own cattle was grazing in among this herd of Texans, so we decided to separate them by the usual method. We rode casually up until we got within a hundred yards of the bunch around the sod house and, making a run for the herd, we let out a couple of war whoops and fired a few rounds from our six-shooters over their heads. It had the desired results, and then some. Just as we came around the corner of the cabin, the four walls began to disintegrate all around us practically falling on our heads. It seems that a dozen or so of the longhorns had gone into the partly completed sod house through an open doorway and, becoming frightened at our shots and the stampeding cattle outside, had come out of that pile of sod in all directions. Wild cattle poured out the one door and every window opening. Since their spread of horns was wider than the window openings, and two or three were trying to get through the same opening at the same time, they leveled the sod shanty to the ground, many pairs of horns being decorated with sod squares as they fled down the valley. The next time I saw the homesteader he and some friends were constructing a new cabin on his claim, but this time it was built of newly cut pine logs.

We continued our journey on down to the river, arriving at a friend's ranch about dusk. As the next day was Sunday, we were invited to stop over for the day and attend a new Mormon Sunday School being held in a nearby log schoolhouse. The Sunday School class was well attended by all ages. The teacher was recently from a little Utah mining town and reminded me of pictures I had seen of Poker Alice and Calamity Jane; however, she had a most kindly heart and knew her Bible perfectly. During the service she had the habit of going to the window every few minutes and leaning far out over the sill for a moment, after which she would return and continue her class. After many trips to the window I became curious to know what she was looking at so often. So, I tiptoed out of the door in the rear of the schoolhouse and stood outside for a moment. I saw nothing unusual to attract attention, but soon the lady again stuck her head out of the window and ejected a quid of chewing tobacco out of her mouth that would have choked a cow.

The next day, we proceeded north down the river toward the Missouri. We had ridden perhaps a couple of hours, crossing and recrossing the Musselshell at shallow fords, when we heard a rifle shot up ahead of us. We thought nothing of the incident, as there was lots of big game in the vicinity and a rancher could shoot a deer in his own dooryard almost any morning. However, as we rode on a little way, another shot rang out in the morning stillness and a couple of twigs fell from the cottonwood tree above us. We saw no one, so cautiously rode on. A few minutes later, around a bend in the river we came into sight of a ranch house and buildings. As we neared the corrals another shot rang out and a bullet whined just over our heads. We stopped short just as a woman came out from behind a nearby tree with a Winchester in her hands. She looked at us for a moment and then said, "Excuse me boys, I thought you were the gang who keep leaving my gates down."

"That's perfectly O. K. lady," Lone Eagle chimed in, "Think nothing of it."

She explained that the neighbor boys had the habit of riding through her ranch, letting down the gates, and never closing them again after passing through. This is truly a breach of range etiquette, as all ranchers know, and we didn't blame her too much for her attitude. We recognized her as Hattie Bell, the tobacco-chewing Sunday-school teacher, better known as the Cattle Queen of the Musselshell.

During the forty-five to fifty miles from Cat Creek to the mouth of the Musselshell we forded the river not less than twenty times. This scenic road follows the river bottom land and changes in many places every spring after the ice goes out. Many ranch buildings may be seen nestled in cozy cottonwood groves along the river. In one place we counted scores of tepee poles, still up, where, not many years before, stood the camp of some roving band of Indian trappers or buffalo hunters.

When we reached the wide, flat bottom lands, where the Musselshell empties into the Missouri we could see a few old foundation rocks where once stood old Fort Musselshell, famous in early frontier steamboat days. As it was now dusk, we decided to camp for the night. After supper we picked out a level, grassy place for our bedroll and tramped over the ground to locate any sticks or small rocks that might be under our blankets. As we did so we picked a slight rise in the ground for the head of our bed. When I opened my eyes the next morning I was staring at a weather-beaten wooden slab. I took a closer look. It was a grave marker. Our slightly raised natural pillow was an old grave mound. We found another grave and marker nearby, also the remains of a wooden picket fence, which one day had enclosed the two lonely graves. Livestock had, no doubt, rubbed the fence and markers down many years before. The markers were flat on the ground, broken, and partly covered with sand and grass. We carefully fitted the old broken pieces together and copied the two hand-carved headboards. After nearly forty years I still have the piece of birch bark on which I copied the inscriptions. They tell their own tragic story.

Here lies

Constant Quenell, Pvt. Co. B. — Inf.
Montreal, Canada. Killed by Indians.

May 24, 1863.

Here lies

William Lehr. Killed by Indians.

Oct. — 1871.

From here we followed the Missouri toward the west. The left or southern bank of the river begins to get rugged west of the Musselshell. The north bank gradually slopes out into a wide plain, forming many large stretches of low bottom lands. The main channel here changes with almost every spring thaw. Many old channels, once plied by the great river boats of seventy-five years ago, are now two miles from the present river bed. Not many years ago, Lone Eagle and I discovered the rusty smokestack and cables of one of these old packet boats protruding from the grassy prairie flats fully one-half mile from the present river channel. Several old river boat hulls have been located far from the present channel.

An almost unbelievable incident took place some years ago in connection with the cargo of one of these old river boats. Records show that one of the old packets was on its way from St. Louis to Fort Benton, loaded with merchandise for the gold camps of Montana. Due to the ever-changing channel, this boat ran aground on a bar of sharp rocks in the middle of the stream, and sank in water up to the pilot house. The crew and passengers were all taken ashore but most of the cargo was submerged and never recovered.

Years later, when the river was very low in the late fall, some woodchoppers located the old boat, which had become partly imbedded in dry sand near the edge of the, then, main stream. Being curious, they spent several days digging about the old decks. Finally they broke into one of the storage rooms where flour had been stored in hundred-pound cotton sacks. This flour had been under water for many years, but was more or less protected from the ravages of the river and, strange to say, most of it was still in usable condition. The water had penetrated the tightly packed sacks to a depth of only three or four inches, thereby forming an air- and water-tight cover of thick dough around each sack, which sealed in the remainder of the flour, preserving it in its original condition. Several tons of perfectly good flour was recovered from this submerged boat. One of these sacks of flour later was sent to the museum at Helena, Montana, and is still on exhibit there.

For many miles along the river the bluffs rise to a height of from two to three hundred feet and in most places they

SCENIC WONDERS IN THE BADLANDS

are nearly perpendicular. They are formed of white sandstone, which is sufficiently soft to wash away easily. Two
or three narrow, horizontal strata of white stone of harder
quality, on which the rains make no noticeable impression,
are imbedded in these cliffs of soft stone near the upper part,
and above this the earth is dark surface gravel. The surface
water, in descending from these hills and plains, has trickled
down the soft sand cliffs and worn them into a thousand gro-
tesque figures, which, with a little imagination, make them
look very much like elegant rows of twenty-story buildings,
having their parapets faced with white marble statuary. Columns, both grooved and plain, appear to be supporting long
carved galleries in front of these richly decorated buildings.
Some of these columns rise from the water's edge to a height
of two to three hundred feet with their pedestals and capitals
complete, while some lie prostrate and broken. They seem
as if built by the hand of man and are so numerous that they
appear like the ruins of some great city. Their grandeur is
far beyond description of my humble pen.

Some thirty miles west of the mouth of the Musselshell is
located the site of one of the early-day boat landings that
served much of the Judith Basin country and even a large
part of the mining camps along Alder Gulch. This landing
was known as Carroll City and consisted of a dozen or so log
cabins and a large warehouse. Leading from the landing into
the Judith Basin and upper Musselshell River country was
the Carroll Trail, over which the Diamond R Freight Company sent its heavily laden wagons.

Lone Eagle and I spent several weeks in this little known
badlands country, scouting and locating landmarks of early-
day Montana history. During hundreds of miles of riding
along the river and following small streams and deep canyons
on either side, we saw less than a dozen human habitations,
mostly along the river banks. There was wild game of every
description.

In one cabin I was shown a most unusual legal document.
An old, tan, battered cowboy hat — the signed will of a dying

cowboy. It seems that a local cowboy rancher had been up in the hills looking after his stock when along a narrow trail his horse had shied or slipped off the ledge and came tumbling down a long, steep embankment, rider and all. A shotgun, which he was carrying on his horse, had discharged into the side of the rider. The wound was serious and the cowboy was alone and far from home or other habitation. His chances of reaching aid were slim and he evidently realized his situation. His horse was found a few days later standing outside his corral gate, lame and badly cut up. The saddle also showed signs of deep rock scratches and clay dirt. His neighbors immediately got up a searching party and, with the assistance of an old half-breed Cree scout, they finally found the object of their search. Not far away was the discharged shotgun, and, lying within arm's length, was his hat, on the wide brim of which he had scrawled: "I am dying   accident   please give all I own to my sister — — Kansas City, Mo.   Albert." The old Stetson hat is still owned by his sister in Kansas City, and a photograph of it is somewhere in the Fergus County records.

Another, less tragic, occurrence took place at a lonely ranch house farther up the river, a couple of days before we arrived. Just back of the house was a smoldering heap of ruins, and during the evening meal we were told of the burning incident. It seems that Junior, then about six years old, had been sent out to the barn by his mother to gather some eggs. He found a few, but evidently not the required number. In an empty stall he saw some more eggs under a hen. However, the hen was in no mood to give up her nest to Junior, no matter how much he shooed her. The hen got a little rough and nipped a couple of fingers. About that time, Junior remembered how he and his father had smoked a bobcat out of a hollow log a few days before, and this gave him an idea. So he lit a match under the unsuspecting hen and her nest. Junior's little smoke-out cost one dozen nearly hatched eggs, forty tons of new-mown hay, four new sets of harness, one thousand bushels of grain, two wagons, and a sixty-foot log barn — and Junior needed a new seat in his old Levis.

One evening we were camping with two cowboys who were out looking for their stock which was ranging in the neighboring hills. It may or may not have been Monday, but they decided it was wash day, and their idea of doing the family wash was unique. They simply took an empty gunny sack, placed a small rock in the bottom, and placed their clothes in the sack with a couple of slices of laundry soap. Tying their lariat around the top, they went down to a bend in the river and suspended the sack in the swift current, completely submerged. The next morning one of the boys hauled the sack out of the river, wrung out the clothes and draped them over the rocks to dry in the sun. Those clothes were perfectly washed and rinsed as neatly as any motor-driven washer could do it. The rock in the bottom of the sack kept it submerged in the rapid current; the clothes and soap whirled around until the soap was dissolved, after which the contents were thoroughly rinsed and ready to be hung up to dry. No buttons missing and no dishpan hands.

Some days later we stopped in at their ranch to spend the night. Several of the boys had discussed whether the proverbial saying, "tough as a boiled owl" was really true. A couple of days before our arrival, one of the boys had shot a large hoot owl out of the top of a tall tree with his six-shooter. Someone suggested they decide for themselves, once and for all, whether owl meat was of the palatable variety. The owl was properly prepared and put in the pot. It was to be kept boiling from 6:00 A. M. to 6:00 P. M., exactly twelve hours. We were invited to decide as to the truth of the saying. And for public information, I do not hesitate to be quoted as saying that no other meat, wearing fur or feathers, could ever be as tough as that boiled owl.

As the fall days shortened and the nights became colder, we began our return journey to Eagle Bar Ranch by way of the old Carroll Trail, which can yet be followed in many places by the deep ruts made by the heavy freight wagons of three quarters of a century ago. We followed this old trail until we came to the foothills of the Judith Mountains, from where we followed Box Elder Creek down toward the Mussel-shell. While riding down along the north bank of Box Elder we found the remains of an old Red River cart, a relic of the Cree half-breed migration into the Judith Basin country in the early 1880's. Hundreds of these old hand-made, two-wheel, wooden carts creaked and groaned behind their slowly moving cattle as the first half-breeds crossed the divide to the new-found grazing lands of central Montana. Very few of these old relics of early transportation are to be seen anywhere today. Although they never quite enjoyed the romantic and picturesque part played by the early freighter teams, the Pony Express, and the famous old Concord stagecoaches, they nevertheless took a most dramatic and important part in the settlement of our great northwestern empire.

Chapter XX

Red Man's Supreme Mystery

THE LAST BATTLE EVER ENGAGED IN BY THE SIOUX WAS BECAUSE of a gross misunderstanding and misinterpretation of a religious tribal dance — miscalled the Ghost Dance or the Messiah Craze — which took place on Wounded Knee Creek on the Pine Ridge reservation in South Dakota, and has become known as the Battle of Wounded Knee.

So to explanation. Consult history and there comes the story of a strange and unknown being who, in 1890, incited the Indians to rebellion; who, in personification of Jesus Christ, gave the promise that once again the prairies should be the Happy Hunting Grounds of the red man, where again would roam the elk, the antelope, and the buffalo, and that the white man would vanish into the eastern seas. Consult history and it tells the story of how the representatives of the many Indian tribes from Canada to Oklahoma journeyed to Pyramid Lake, Nevada, that they might hear a message of war and hatred; of how the ghost shirt, supposedly impervious to bullets, was fashioned, and particularly of how it was Short Bull, of the Sioux, who spread the news and brought about the war which followed.

Therefore, it was because of this history and the added fact that I had been told by my brother, Lone Eagle, and several of the old warriors who had participated in this new religious dance and the Battle of Wounded Knee, that I sought out a quiet little man then living far out upon the Sioux reservation of Pine Ridge. The man whom we visited that day was Short Bull, blamed for a quarter of a century for an Indian war which called forth half the troops of the United States, and cost the lives of hundreds — this war of the Messiah. And this little man of the Sioux that we found was blamed for it all, yet he had always denied that he caused a war. And so it was, on that autumn afternoon in 1915, that Lone Eagle and I heard from the lips of Short Bull himself of how it was peace he preached and sought, and not the war for which he was blamed.

"There was starvation in 1888 and 1889," he said slowly. "The tepees were cold for want of fires. Up on the Rosebud agency where I lived we cried for food, as they did down here at Pine Ridge. The white man had forgotten us. We were going toward the sunset. Then, one day — it seemed we all heard it at once — there came a message that the Messiah was soon to come to us. The white man had turned him out, long ago. Now he was coming to the Indian. We danced for joy — the dance of the Messiah. This Messiah perhaps would bring us food and warmth and clothing. There was a message, too, from Red Cloud on Pine Ridge. Red Cloud said, too, that the Messiah was coming and to choose a brave-hearted man of the tribe to meet him. I was that man.

"There were several of us, each from a different tribe. One by one we traveled to the head of Wind River and met. The Messiah was in Nevada at Pyramid Lake. Some of us had horses. Others walked. We did not care for fatigue or for hunger. One must suffer to see God. We traveled on. We finally reached Pyramid Lake. And then — some way we all knew where he would come and when he would come, at sunset by the great rocks. So we waited. I had not believed. They had taught me in the parish churches not to believe too much. So I stood there and watched and looked here and there to see where he would come from. I looked hard and I rubbed my eyes. He had not come at all. He was there. Just as if he had floated through the air.

"He was the Holy Man. His gown was like fire. It caught the sun rays and sent them back to the west. It glowed like the fire of a feast. It changed colors. All over the robe there were crosses, from his head to his feet. Some of them were in white — some were in red. We could not see much, for when he looked at us we were afraid and closed our eyes. He raised his arms and there seemed to be fire all about him. We fell down and worshipped. And when we raised our heads he was gone.

"We did not talk much. We were afraid. The next morning a little white boy came to us and told us his father was ready to see us and talk to us down in the willow grove by the lake. You see — the Messiah had a little boy," declared Short Bull. "The little boy said the Messiah was his father. So we went to the willow patch, and he was there, just as we had seen him the night before. He talked to all of us, but he talked to me the most. He came close to me. He laid his hand on my fore- head and I thought that fire had gone through me. He held my hands and they turned numb. His hands were hot when they touched me. When they left me they were cold — cold like the wind outside. Then he talked.

" 'A long time ago,' he said, and he talked as if it hurt to remember, 'I came among the white people. But they did not like me. They sent me away. They crucified me.' "

Short Bull then raised his hands and pointed to his palms. He raised his beaded-moccasined feet and pointed there. He bared his breast and patted it above his heart.

"He was the *Holy* Man, I saw. He showed me. Here, and here, and here — where they had nailed him on the crucifix! He was the Holy Man!

"But after the Holy Man said that, he smiled and shook his head. That was a long time ago that the white people did that and now he didn't care. Now he had come back to bring peace. 'I have come back,' he said, 'to bring you news. You have fought with the white man. That is wrong. I want you to go back to your tribe and tell them what I have said. You must say that the white man and the Indian shall live in peace. There may be trouble. Stamp it out like a prairie fire. They may try to kill you, Short Bull, and even if they should, do not fight back. You must live in peace. Your children must go to the white man's school and your children's children must grow to become the husbands and wives of the white man and the white woman.

" 'And some day there will be no Indian. There will be no white man. You will all be one, and then will be peace. Listen to me,' he said, 'and listen to each other. I am the Holy Man. I am the Messiah. Listen to the white man and the white man shall listen to you. Do as I say and on earth you will be together — and in heaven you will be together. And then there shall be no nights, no sleeps, no hunger, no cold. You shall be with me! You have come unto me,' the Holy Man said, 'to learn the news. I have told it to you and now you must journey forth to tell it to the others who wait by the tepees. Tell them to be merciful unto each other. Tell them the Father says to do no harm, but to live in peace.' And he told this to each one of us. To me he told it in Sioux. He told it to the others in their own language. Could any man but God have done it? There is no man who can talk all the languages. He taught us to dance and he says this is the dance we must perform. He showed us his robe and told us that we should worship him by wearing robes like this. He told us that we must throw away the rifle and the war club.

" 'Live in peace,' he said, 'and let the white man live in peace with you.'

"And that was all he said. Pretty soon he was gone and we turned and came home. Yes, that was all. I went home — and all before me there was singing and happiness. They had heard of the Messiah. All down through Pine Ridge they sang and danced, and pretty soon Red Cloud, Fast Thunder, American Horse, and Sitting Bull sent for me to come home. I knew what they wanted. They wanted war. They did not want to do as the Holy Man said. And so I went. I talked to them and they laughed at me. Then they brought me the ghost shirts to bless. I blessed them — and then they went back to their people and told them I had said that bullets would not pierce the ghost shirts. They went back and told their people I had brought a new message from the Messiah, but that I could not give it directly. They told their people I had said the white man was to be driven out and that there must be war. But I did not know then. When I heard it was too late. All through the reservations they were dancing now — and dancing for war — because American Horse, Fast Thunder, Rain-in-the-Face, Red Cloud, and Sitting Bull wanted war. They had blamed it all on me — and yet I only told what the Messiah had ordered me to tell. I begged them to listen to the Holy Man — to hear the news he had sent and live in peace with the white man. I did not want war; I did not want it! The Messiah had told me what to do and I was trying to do it.

"I had told my people we should dance for the Messiah when the grass turned brown, but the police from the agency came out and told me to stop. Then they told me the soldiers were coming. And then Fast Thunder, American Horse, Red Cloud, and Sitting Bull called for me to come to Pine Ridge and fight the white man. But I said 'No! No! The Messiah has said there must be no war.' Old Two Strikes moved his camp from the Little White River toward Pine Ridge, but I stayed. The Brules moved from the Rosebud toward Pine Ridge, but still I stayed. I had seen the Holy Man and he had told me to live in peace. Then the young men of the Rosebud came to me and ordered me to follow Two Strikes. I followed. They talked to me about guns and ammunition, but I would not help them get them. I did not want war; I wanted to do what the Messiah had told me. We went to the Badlands. They told me that now I must fight against the white men. 'No! No!' I cried out to them: 'No!' I kept calling; 'You do do not hear me. I do not want to fight against the white man! The Messiah says, " 'There shall be no more war; but you will not listen.' "

" 'Once I was a warrior, once I wore the shield and the war

club and the war bonnet; but I have seen the Holy Man. Now is peace; now there shall stay peace. You chose me as the brave-hearted one to journey to the sunset to see the Messiah. I saw him, and I brought you his message. You would not hear it. You changed it. " 'Now ——' " he said, 'I am silent.' "

"The next day I saddled my horse. I rode away. I came to the pine hills and looked out in the distance. They were fighting the Battle of Wounded Knee. I kept on. They fought the battle of the Missions, and they blame me for it — me, who saw the Holy Man. They were jealous; I was a brave-hearted man, and I was a chief. They did not like me; so they blame me for a war — my own people, my people who had sent me to the sunset that I might talk to Him, the Holy Man!"

So there is the story of Short Bull, whatever history may say. This is the story told me by that wrinkled little heart-broken old Indian who, that day, was reliving the past, standing there in the sunset along the shores of Pyramid Lake, listening to the message of the Messiah.

Not many years after my visit to Short Bull's lodge on the Pine Ridge, I spent a summer on the placid shores of the picturesque Pyramid Lake in Nevada, where I had heard of an old man of the Piute tribe who claimed to have also witnessed the coming of this so-called Messiah, on the rocky shore of this Lake of the Pyramid. His story was almost identical to that which was related to me by Short Bull, but he saw material things there that day in the rocks that were apparently missed by the little man of the Sioux, from whose explanation came the first glimpse of the truth about the so-called Messiah.

This man of the Messiah had come to the land of the Piute on the shores of the lake in a wagon sometime before and made a camp behind the big rocks. It had been seen by this tribesman of the Piutes. This person who desired to portray the part of a Messiah, was perhaps some small-town, street-corner orator, whose knowledge of the superstition of the Indian, and who was inspired by a will and desire to be a prophet and a messenger of peace to the Indian people, had proposed a great scheme, with the spirit of the faker to carry it through. With the brilliant rays of the setting sun shining on his changeable silken robe — and by his spectacular act of leaping out from behind a small shelf in the rocks, he appeared to float through the air to the place viewed by the waiting assembly of Indians. Thus they had seen with their own eyes and believed. Believed and worshipped with all the superstition and all the faith of the Indian race, worshipped a man in a changeable silken robe, who had mysteriously come to them along the shores of the Lake of the Pyramid in the brilliant sunset of the West.

THE PROPHECY OF AN AMERICAN INDIAN

I stand in the dying sunset,
And mine is a vanishing race;
Now hearken to me, you white man,
As I meet you, again, face to face.

My fathers were they who first met you,
Where the tides of the Great Waters flow;
Far, far to the east as the arrow flies,
Ten thousand moons ago.

My fathers who ranged through the forests,
My fathers by river and sea;
Who roamed through their vast dominions
Like the winds of the heavens, as free.

They were brothers to storm, and the sunshine,
They were brothers to oak and the pine;
They were shadows that stole with moccasined feet,
Through the glades where the wild grapes twine.

And they hunted the deer and the turkey,
The wolf and the fox and the bear;
They fished in the brooks and the rivers
And they speared the great salmon there.

No fear of the lightning's terrors,
No fear of the wolf's hunger cry;
Where the smoke of their many wigwams
Wheeled calmly against the sky.

So lived my fathers, Oh, pale face!
They were children of vast and of wild,
They were happy within their borders
In a land that was undefiled.

Then, one day, from over the waters
A speck loomed dark 'gainst the sky;
And shadows ran swift through the forest,
Where the night owl hooted its cry.

And my fathers went down to your fathers,
While the keel grated harsh on the sand;
And they welcomed your fathers, Oh, pale face,
With the pipe of peace in their hand.

So the moons went by in succession,
And greater your people grew;
And far was the smoke of their wigwams,
While back in the forests we drew.

Then we saw that our lands were taken,
And the greed where your footsteps led,
And our faith in your fathers was shaken,
And we fought and together we bled.

But vain was the terror of war-whoop,
And your scalps held high in our hand;
For ever the smoke of your wigwams
Spread farther throughout the land.

And ever we fled before it,
While the forests were lined with our dead,
And we turned our face towards the westward
To the land where the sun burns red.

Then you fought with the sons of your mother,
Her sons who came over the sea;
Who would crush the hopes of your future
And strangle your liberty.

But you threw them across the far waters
To the land of the rising sun;
And again you builded your empire
With the fruits of your victory won.

Then peace and then wars in succession,
And the moons they were bloody with strife,
While out of the throes of rebellion
You welded your national life.

And so you waxed strong in your power,
While your muscles were knitted of steel,
And the world bowed low in her homage,
As she came to your footstools to kneel.

Then you threw back your wide, golden portals,
High lifted your liberty's torch;
And over the sea came a tidal wave
Of millions that crowded your porch.

And you set them to dig in your ditches,
This brood of an alien race.
While you lifted your cup to pleasure
And toasted her painted face.

Then wealth poured into your coffers,
And it flowed in a golden tide;
While you drank the wine of your madness,
Drank deep of your power and pride.

And your daughters cared not to be mothers,
For papooses, cared not, on their knee.
And trained in your schools of learning
From such shackles they fain would be free.

So they grew to be independent,
For who would be tied to a home,
When the jazz and the dance were calling,
And the white lights where they might roam.

Now they go about in their motors,
Or with a Pekinese tied to a string;
Far better a tour with Baedecker
Than a child in the world to bring.

While lone on New England hillsides,
Stand your homes of Colonial pride,
Whose children have gone to the cities,
Whose fathers and mothers have died.

And ever the tide grew larger,
The tide with the alien cry;
While deeper you drank to your madness,
And higher the cup lifted high.

So you bartered away your birthright,
For the pottage of pleasure and lust,
The birthright your fathers had died for,
Your heritage held in their trust.

Then one day you woke from your stupor,
And rose from your orgy and feast;
And saw on the west coast the brown man,
And a dark skinned one on your east.

And you saw the tide of their children,
As it broke on your own barren shore!
Then you lifted your voice in terror,
And you slammed in their faces your door.

And you read on your wall the handwriting,
And the letters were large and plain;
In one body you next tried to fuse them,
But your melting pot melted in vain.

And some there be that are vipers,
While with hatred their eyes now burn,
You have taken them into your bosom,
And deep they shall strike in return.

For hearken you Anglo-Saxon,
Though your belching guns may boom,
You shall follow our father's footsteps
And your remnant shall march to its doom.

You shall stand with us in the sunset,
You shall follow our dying race;
In the house that your fathers builded,
An alien shall stand in your place.

Ah, well for your closed eastern portals,
For your well guarded Golden Gate.
But I from the shores of the spirit land
Shall mock you and cry — Too late!

Chapter XXI

Looking Back Over the Years

DURING THE SUMMER OF 1915, LONE EAGLE AND I TOOK A LONG-
planned trip back to the home of our parents in Sussex
County, New Jersey. Many times I had told my brother the
story of our parents and their journey to the West and of how
he was left, an orphan, among the Sioux.

The family of Jacob Maine had been numerous in the
peaceful little village of Stillwater, along the Paulins Kill, and
many descendants were still to be found living in the same
stately old homes of their ancestors. Many of them still remembered the young missionary and his wife who ventured into
the little known land of the Dakotas more than twenty-five
years before. We met many with our family name. All were
greatly interested in the romantic story of Lone Eagle and his
adventurous boyhood days, and of our eventful meeting in the
Indian country along the Little Big Horn. Our broad-
brimmed hats, high-heeled boots and general Western attire
were quite a curiosity among our Eastern relatives.

Lone Eagle never quite got used to the maze of tall buildings in the big cities and he was always a little frightened at
the multitude of ever-rushing people and the noisy traffic of
the busy streets. Even I, after so many years away from the
noise and bustle of the metropolitan areas of my birthplace,
was not a little uneasy when among the now unfamiliar

crowds. We stayed for several weeks and, in September, bade our many friends and relatives adieu, and began our homeward journey. We stopped a few days to see White Fawn, who had just returned for her last year at Carlisle. She had now grown into a most charming and talented young lady. She and Lone Eagle planned to get married following a year of teaching at the Agency school in Montana. We also visited the home of Big Elk and Cloud Woman in whose lodge Lone Eagle had lived as a boy. Many winters had silvered their hair noticeably and they were overjoyed at our coming to see them. They truly loved Lone Eagle as their own son.

We had heartily enjoyed our visit among our friends and relatives but were happy to be back among familiar surroundings and the quiet of the great outdoors. However, soon after we had settled down to our daily ranching routine, war clouds began to appear in the land along the Rhine. Soon we and many of our friends were laying away our spurs and saddles for the olive-drab tunics and campaign hats. It was not until mid-summer of 1919 that we once more resumed our ranching.

White Fawn had continued her teaching during the years that Lone Eagle was in uniform and they were married at our ranch home on December 11, 1919, just forty years — to a day — after the wedding of our own parents in the old Bonnie Brook family mansion in Sussex County. Many moons have come and gone since those early homesteading days on Eagle Bar Ranch but they will never be forgotten.

Not long ago while on a visit in Lewistown, I chanced to meet a couple of my old Army buddies. Usually, when old friends meet, they recall some incident of bygone days. It so happened that this chap and I were tentmates for several months before the old One Hundred Sixty-third Montana sailed for the European war zone. In December, 1917, our outfit was camped in Mineola, Long Island, waiting for orders to sail overseas. In our tent squad, besides this fellow and myself, were Lone Eagle and five cowboys from the Powder River country. A more congenial lot of boys were never housed together under one Sibley squad tent. The One Hundred

Sixty-third was made up of boys from Montana, with a few replacements from Wyoming and a couple of other Western states.

The Montana cow country and several Indian reservations were well represented in our outfit. We were the first Western troops to arrive in Mineola, and since some of our boys had not yet been issued regulation uniforms, there were plenty of high-heeled cowboy boots, ten-gallon hats, beaded moccasins, and long black braids seen on our company streets. Most of the cowboys and Indians were quite crestfallen when issued their first pair of army shoes.

The squad tent was standard housing equipment, and was rather cramped for the boys from the wide-open spaces. Lone Eagle, having lived most of his life among the plains Indians, was quite used to tepee life and the old Sibley was about the only camp equipment that reminded him of his early home. However, one thing was missing. The Indians were in the habit of painting their tents with colorful designs, including their personal and family histories, in Indian picture writing above and around the tepee door.

Some one in our tent procured a box of wax lumber crayons in deep red, blue, and black, and the rest of the squad proudly looked on while Lone Eagle spent the better part of a forenoon painting the family crest and Indian totems all over our new canvas abode. The sketches consisted of buffalo, horses, Indians, cowboys, and Sioux hieroglyphic picture writing. The carefully sketched subjects were really a commendable piece of Indian and cowboy art — a colorful paint job worthy of a Russell's approval. To add to the array on our gaily painted domicile, the rest of the occupants decided they should make known their residence in the tepee by adding their own trademarks and signatures to the already well-covered canvas. So it was not long until the rest of the exterior of our Army home was a maze of monograms and cattle brands of our family squad of eight.

Our popularity soon exceeded our fondest expectations; everyone on our company street came by to admire our artistic display. We had painted ourselves into the limelight, which lasted until that afternoon, when the regimental colonel and his staff held a company inspection in all company streets, and we were viewed in front of our respective tents. We slicked up the interior in double time and were soon ready and waiting for the worthy mass of braid and silverware. At 3:45 he and his staff walked leisurely up the long street to our squad and suddenly stopped and looked, long and hard, but not at us. It was our gaily painted tent that attracted his attention. He took a couple of steps in our direction and yelled out, "Who did that?" For a moment we were so startled that no one answered. Again, pointing to our tent, he yelled: "I say, did you hear me, Who did that?" so loudly we nearly bounced off our feet. Lone Eagle, not sure whether he was to be fired or promoted to company commander, grinned and answered, "Me Sir, from Powder River, let 'er buck!" The colonel looked stern for a moment and then broke into a long grin, as he continued: "You will be excused at once to remove the art paintings from your canvas if you have to drain Powder River to do so." However, the entire squad procured soap and brushes from the company kitchen and put on a scrubbing bee, soon removing our display of Western art from Uncle Sam's war tepee.

Life has not always been easy on the Western plains, but we who knew and lived it offer no complaints. I have seen thousands of acres of golden grain waiting only for another day of ripening sunshine before the harvest, when suddenly the sky above was clouded over by myriads of locusts so thick they blotted out the sun. Forty-eight hours later the fields were a blanket of crawling grasshoppers and not a blade of grass or grain could be seen for miles around. Again, I have waited only for the morrow to begin the harvest of a field of waving grain, so heavy it would easily sustain a hat as though floating on a surface of water. In an hour, a threatening black cloud appeared, and before I could reach cover, hailstones beat the waving grain into the earth until it was as clean and bare as a baseball field.

I have seen the roaring, raging winter blizzard blow the biting icy snow into our faces until it cut like flakes of steel. I have struggled and floundered against stinging blasts of swirling snow in midday so dark and dense we held hands so as not to lose sight of each other at less than three paces, and our voices carried no farther. Even to breathe was frozen torture.

But the winter does not hold all the danger and horrors of the great unfenced prairies. I shall never forget a roaring, racing prairie fire that nearly cost the lives of my brother and me and a cowboy friend. Caught on the flaming front of a three-mile-wide prairie grass fire, we were forced to race ahead of a forty-mile wind, and at no time were we ever more than two hundred yards ahead of the leaping flames. To turn to the right or left would serve only to lessen our distance from the ten-foot wall of flame. For nearly seven miles we raced for our very lives, hoping and trusting only to God and the fleetness and surefootedness of our wiry mustangs. Nearing an old buffalo wallow, we made for it, and taking advantage of its bare, dry mud bed, we hastily set a backfire along the nearest edge and rushed for the opposite side, where we lay down with our faces to the ground, until the fire swept around us not a hundred feet away. But these were the exceptions. More common were the years of plenty, when our ranges were filled with thousands of fat cattle, and golden grain waved in the gentle breeze as far as the eye could see.

In looking back over the years, the succession of unusual events has made the story of our lives seem like a dream — a page out of a book of fantastic fairy tales. Two brothers, sons of the same parents, one born and raised in the center of Eastern culture; the other born in a tepee and brought up as an Indian on the great Western plains, after years of living in different worlds and environments, at last met under circumstances almost unbelievable. We continued our lives together in perfect harmony and understanding, each always admiring the association and experiences of the other.

Inheritance and environment have silently and surely

played a strange and interesting part in our lives. My brother never quite outgrew or forgot his early training among the Sioux. His adopted people were always closest to his heart. His early environment and the love of his kindly adopted family played a part which was never erased from his nature. He realized his birthright but by nature he always was an Indian at heart. His love, admiration, and consideration for his adopted people were reflected in the numerous friends of his youth. To them, he was as much an Indian as though never a drop of white blood ran through his veins. They taught him all that they would have taught their own sons. They sought his counsel as though he were a member of their highest tribunal. They bestowed upon him the love, affection, and trust that is accorded only to their closest blood brothers. In turn, he was ever loyal to their trust and sincerest friendship.

Each year as the maple leaves fell in the autumn, he made a pilgrimage to the land of his birth to see, once more, his adopted people. Many of the white man's houses now dot the prairies where once he knew only the low-lying lodges and big white tepees of his people. He went from lodge to lodge looking for the friends he once knew, but the Indians of his boyhood came to greet him no more. Their campfires are burning for him among the sand hills in the Happy Hunting Grounds. So ends my story.